GRIEF

It's NOT Supposed To Be OK!

D1714700

Skinner & Kirk

Copyright

GRIEF - It's NOT Supposed To Be OK!

© 2021 by Ron Skinner & Jeff Kirk.

All Rights Reserved.

All rights reserved. No part of this book may be reproduced in any form or by any electronic or mechanical means, including information storage and retrieval systems, without permission in writing from the author. The only exception is by a reviewer, who may quote short excerpts in a review, and as permitted by U.S. copyright law...

Although the author and publisher have made every effort to ensure that the information in this book was correct at press time, the author and publisher do not assume and hereby disclaim any liability to any party for any loss, damage, or disruption caused by errors or omissions, whether such errors or omissions result from negligence, accident, or any other cause.

Some names and identifying details have been changed to protect the privacy of individuals.

The information in this book is meant to supplement, not replace, proper grief counseling.

Table of Contents

Copyright.. 3

Dedication... 11

Foreword.. 13

Preface 15

The Author's Commitment to You...................................... 17

Introduction 19

Understanding There Is No Wrong Way to Grieve................. 25

Understanding That Your Grief is Unique............................ 27

Understanding Grief Has No Time Limit 29

Stages... Really?... 31

Where Did "The Five Stages of Grief" Come From? 33

The Five Stages 34

Stage One: Denial 34

Stage Two: Anger.. 35

Stage Three: Bargaining....................................... 36

Stage Four: Depression 36

Stage Five: Acceptance 38

Could there be A Sixth Stage? 39

So, How Do We Cope? 41

Signs of Complicated Grief.................................. 49

Major, or Clinical, Depression 51

When to Get Help 53

What Coping Does Not Mean 57

Coping does not mean being "strong."............... 57

Secondly, coping does not always mean crying. 57

Coping does not mean experiencing all five stages of grief.
.... 58

Coping does not mean you are done grieving. 58

Finding Your Way Now... 59

Recognize you are Grieving................................ 60

Common Grief Reactions 61

Physical Reactions 61

Spiritual Reactions 63

Emotional Reactions 63

Cognitive Reactions.. 65

Behavioral Reactions.. 66

Don't forget that your Children are grieving too! 67

What About You?.. 71

Combating the Mind 72

Protecting Your Body 73

Outward Struggles of Grief 77

How to Deal with Your Loved One's Possessions? 77

Dealing with the Family and Friends 79

Seeing Your Loved One in Unexpected Places 79

The Hurdles of Special Days.. 80

So.... What to Do? 81

Inward Struggles of Grief 83

You're Suffering More Than One Loss 83

Struggles... and More Struggles 85

Feelings of Relief.. 85

The Blame Game.. 88

Guilt... 88

Regret... 89

Misplaced Guilt and Self Punishment............................. 91

The Struggle of Resentment 95

Tears and Strength.. 99

Isolation and Loneliness 101

Understanding Isolation 103

Social Isolation 103

Emotional Isolation 103

Loneliness... 104

The Risks of Loneliness and Isolation from Others 104

Combating Loneliness and Isolation 105

Overcoming... 105

The Fallacy of Closure 109

What Is Closure? 109

Our Uneasy Truce with Grief 109

Expecting Closure is Inviting Disappointment 111

"Healing" Without Closure.. 112

Moving on in Your Grief.. 113

Moving On "In" Not Moving On "From"........................... 113

Others Do Not Define When You Move On 113

You Define When You Will "Move On".............................. 114

We Move on but Never Forget 114

It Does Not Mean Grief Will End...................................... 115

Does Time Heal all Wounds? 115

What Now? 117

Accept Your Emotions.. 117

Focus on One Day at a Time 117

Find Meaning in Your Life 117

Talk to a Friend 118

Be a Friend 119

Talk to a Counselor or Grief Coach 119

Continuing the Race 121

Why We Disengage When We Grieve 122

Why Should We Engage? 125

How Do We Engage? 126

Dig Deep 126

Decide on a Strategy 127

What Should be Part of Our Plan? 128

Engaging in a New Life 132

What Will Change? 133

How Do You Deal with Change? 137

People Sometimes say the Most Hurtful Things 143

Two of the most egregious things that were said directly to us were as follows: 144

How to Respond 146

Tell Them How They Can Help 147

Use It as a Learning Experience 147

Specific Relational and Conditional Losses 149

The Loss of a Spouse 149

How NOT to Handle the Loss of a Spouse 151

Enduring Grief 153

The Loss of a Child 155

Losing a Parent 159

Losing a Sibling 160

Suicide 163

National Tragedy 167

Pandemic (COVID-19) 170

Dementia/Alzheimer's 172

Types of Grief 175

Acute Grief 175

Complicated Grief 180

How Is Complicated Grief Treated? 182

Integrated Grief 183

Conclusion 185

Resource and Support Section 189

About the Authors 191

References 193

Dedication

This book is dedicated to all who have loved and lost. Your journey with grief is no doubt long and beyond difficult yet you persevere. Though you may not feel like it, you are stronger than you know.

To Jeff's mom who so valiantly struggled with the loss of her husband leaving her with the unimaginable responsibilities as a young mother that no one should have to bear without their spouse. To my "Pop Pop" who took on much of the role of a father. Thank you for your love and sacrifice. Your impact on my life continues still.

To Ron's mom who struggled throughout life but never wavered in her love and commitment to her boys. You showed me perseverance if not perfection. I have become the person I am today largely because of your example.

Finally, this work is dedicated to all who have found their way here and are looking for understanding and hope as they travel their journey in grief. Be encouraged! The sun will shine again, and life is still worth living!

Foreword

In 2020, America and the entire world would experience a pandemic known as COVID-19, a virus that would change us forever. This virus would cause over 670,000 fatalities in the US alone and 5,550,000 as of September 2021. With numbers this high, the ripple effect of those left behind coping with death and grief is devastating, but there is Hope!

I, too, am a mother whose son was in the military, who had mental illness and took his own life by suicide on August 23, 2016. I was propelled to write a book, *"Forever Twenty-Nine"*, which is a love story of a mother for her son, a son's love for his mother, God's love for me to caterpillar my grief and pain to help others. I understand first-hand the pain and difficult journey of grief and going from mourning to joy!

Ron Skinner & Jeff Kirk have chosen a perfect time to collaborate and share their individual stories with grief under one book, *"GRIEF - It's NOT Supposed To Be OK!."* Ron and Jeff tell us how losing a family member, grandparent, and child will forever impact and change your life. Ron is also very candid (In his soon to be released book) about how his son, who took his own life by suicide, struggled and the ripple effect on those left behind.

Ron and Jeff provide resources to help you on your journey and explain the five stages of grief. The lessons they've learned about grief are invaluable.

"GRIEF - It's NOT Supposed To Be OK!" will give you encouragement and let you know you're not alone on this journey. Your grief is unique to you because of the relationship and the love you shared with that person!

Beloved, grief is something we all must face one day. Use the tools that are provided here, and remember God is with you. You are never alone. Hebrew 12:1 (KJV) "Wherefore seeing we also are compassed about with so great a cloud of witnesses, let us lay aside every weight and the sin which doth so easily beset us, and let us run with patience the race that is set before us."

Kimberly Peatrice

Master Grief Coach

Preface

God Did Not Promise Days Without Pain.

Laughter Without Sorrow, nor Sun Without

Rain, but He Did Promise Strength for the

Day, Comfort for the Tears, and Light for the

Way.

Unknown

Nothing can fix your grief. But then again, is grief something that needs to be "fixed"? Grieving the loss of a loved one can be overwhelming, unimaginable, never-ending, and without a doubt, forever life changing.

This book is for anyone who has loved and lost or who wants to be more supportive of someone that is grieving. The aim of this book is to help you understand what you are feeling, and that grieving is part of love and life. The loss of a loved one is not something to get over. You are forever changed. Your life and how that person fits in it are changed. This does not mean life is not worth living, it is just different. Grief is different for everyone.

As parents, when my wife and I lost a child, I assumed that the loss would be equal for each of the immediate family members. Such assumptions often lead to additional struggles in the family. Many times, one partner cannot understand the grief of others. But that assumption of a parallel level of grief is in error. The mother carried that child in her womb. A father's love for his son and his heir does not equate to a mother's love for the child she carried in her womb. The memories you carry of your sibling with whom you may have shared deep secrets, cannot possibly be understood by your parents. Your unique relationship with the one lost makes your grief unique.

Grief is the inverse of love. To love deeply, one may grieve deeply. And that is OK. We provide insights as to what you are feeling and practical resources to deal with those issues.

The Author's Commitment to You

This book was written from the heart of fellow grievers. As such, there are certain principles to which we have adhered to in the writing of this work on which we were not willing to compromise.

We have been honest, even ruthless at times in presenting Grief as it really is, not as we wish that it were. Even when it might have served the authors better to be a little more encouraging or empathetic, we always erred on the side of truthfulness. Believing that nothing of true value ever comes from anything other than the pure and simple truth.

Grief is a deep, complicated, and immensely painful subject to which we all will likely become accustomed in our lives.

Untold hours of research as well as drawing on the well of experience of our own grief have gone into this book. It is our sincere hope that we might help others as they endure grief.

Introduction

You are not alone in loss. Approximately 150,000 people die every day. Their friends and loved ones suffer grief, loss, and heartbreak. Sometimes, there seems to be no end to the pain. The heartache can feel unbearable.

Those of us who are left behind can experience our grief so profoundly that it can begin to damage both our mental and physical health. We may become irritable, numb, detached, or bitter. We may struggle to experience or show joy or become preoccupied with loss. Grief can affect us so profoundly that it causes fatigue, digestive problems, chest pain, headaches, and a whole host of other problems.

Unfortunately, grief's reach extends far beyond the emotional pain we experience. Often, our loss can result in financial problems stemming from the realities of laying our loved ones to rest and the loss of the ongoing income they may have provided. All of this at the precise time we are least able to make sound financial decisions. This, in turn, can further impact our grief as the struggles of life for the one left behind are an ever-present burden. Some may resort to "retail therapy" to buy away the pain. We live in the buy now and pay later culture; it is as easy to spend money we don't have as it is to breathe. Some may make unwise financial decisions choosing to spend extravagantly on their loved one's final expenses. Often far beyond what they would have wanted. Still, others, perhaps in a need to control something in their out-of-control world, make rash decisions to sell their home or get rid of all their loved one's possessions, only to regret it later. Some of the above may be unavoidable but often leads to unintended consequences later. Your grief may also be affecting your relationships with friends and colleagues. Sometimes, even family may seem to be pulling away, unsure how to respond. As you experience grief, you may withdraw from others, unsure how else to cope.

At this most difficult time, we implore you to think of one or two people you know to be levelheaded and caring. This allows you to call upon a small group of people you trust to talk to about the life-changing decisions you make at such a vulnerable time. Seeking wise counsel can only help.

Is this you? Does any of what you have just read hit home for you? Have you lost your child or a parent? Has your spouse gone on to eternity without you? Have you lost a sibling? Are you struggling, and no one seems to really understand?

You may be wondering how to cope. Or maybe you think you've been grieving for too long or that you're not grieving enough. Perhaps you're wondering when the pain will end. This book, *GRIEF - It's NOT Supposed To Be OK!*, will help you answer these questions.

In this book, you'll learn:

1. There's no wrong way to grieve.
2. Your grief is unique and why.
3. "Closure" is a fantasy. You must learn to live with your loss. We never "get over" loss, but you will learn to live through it.

We understand the depth of your suffering. We know some of the questions you may be facing. and the answers you seek. We have asked the same questions and sought the same answers.

We have both experienced tremendous losses in very unexpected ways. Jeff has seen the effects of grief first-hand. After his father lost his life in a tragic industrial accident when he was 18 months old, his mother spent years on medications just to make it through the days. Even then, his mother was unable to cope, and Jeff was shifted around between his aunt and uncle and his grandfather until he was seven or eight years old. This experience has given him a unique view of loss and the impact it can have.

By the age of 19, Ron had lost both his grandmother and his father. He would eventually marry and have three boys only to lose two of them within an 18-month period These experiences have given the authors tremendous compassion and understanding for the depth of suffering and the difficulty death brings.

We have lived with the aftermath of the death of multiple family members for many years. Our collective experience with grief spans over 80 years, giving us an insight into grief that has created within us a passion for helping others.

We know this thing called grief, this thing that you are experiencing. We are intimately acquainted with it, just as you are becoming familiar with grief now. You and your grief are important to us, and while we don't promise to "make it all better," we can give you some tools to live with and live through your grief.

While your grief is unique to you, each person's grief also involves certain foundational realities. These realities cannot be tied up in a neat little box, but they can be summed up. We'll expound on them more later in the book. First, grief is generally not short-lived and can last a lifetime. Secondly, the struggles of loss will always be with you. Thirdly, however, you can be encouraged! There is hope! While you will never "get over" your loss, you will get through it. You will survive. You can even thrive in this life as you carry the burden of loss.

In this book, GRIEF - It's NOT Supposed To Be OK!, we share our insights into grief and all it entails. Because of our experiences, we can do this with deep empathy and understanding of the unimaginable pain and struggle that accompanies loss. We have written this book hoping that our grief and struggles with death and loss might bring you some comfort in knowing that while you must travel your journey of grief and carry your unique burden alone, others are carrying theirs as well. So, in a very real sense, you are not alone at all. Never has a road been so universally traveled by so many, with each feeling as if they are all alone. Always remember that we really are all in this together though we each grieve in our own way.

Understanding There Is No Wrong Way to Grieve

"Life seems sometimes like nothing more than a series of losses, from beginning to end. That is the given. How you respond to those losses, what you make of what is left, that's the part you have to make up as you go." — Katharine Weber

Grief is often associated with sadness. Such an assumption about the emotions we experience with grief is woefully incomplete. Grief is a combination of emotions and not just one. In grief we feel:

- Sadness
- Anger
- Guilt
- Joy
- Gratitude
- Anxiety
- Relief
- Confusion
- Envy
- Yearning
- Resentment
- Numbness
- Frustration
- Hope
- Fear

With all these emotions and combinations, no one can tell you how to grieve or that you are doing it wrong.

Understanding That Your Grief is Unique

"We live, we love, and we grieve. Only death is more universally experienced than grief. Be that as it may, all grief is as unique as the never-ending snowflakes."

Ron Skinner

Remember Your Grief is Unique - Don't try to compare your grief journey with that of others. Your journey is unique. It's influenced by your unique relationship, experiences shared, circumstances of their death, your religious and cultural background, other losses you've experienced, and so much more. For this reason, it can be so hurtful when others try to show empathy by drawing parallels between your loss and theirs. It is not the same. It never was, and it never will be. How can they possibly understand what you are going through? As stated above, with so many emotions and other variables, it makes sense that grief is unique for everyone.

Think about some of your relationships and compare them to others you know. An example would be twin siblings that lose a parent. All things being equal, time (within a few minutes), and relationship, but that is where the similarities end. Now life experiences start affecting the equation. Just the fact that a daughter may be closer to her mother and a son to his father, or vice versa. Memories and moments shared are different and affect our love and therefore our grief. Future hopes and dreams, for example, will influence how you experience grief. There is simply no way that another human being, no matter how close, can fully understand your grief.

Your hopes and dreams are forever gone. Your life's direction has been irrevocably altered. The question is how do you move on in this new reality?

Understanding Grief Has No Time Limit

"The reality is that you will grieve forever. You will not "get over" the loss of a loved one; you will learn to live with it. You will heal and you will rebuild yourself around the loss you have suffered. You will be whole again but you will never be the same. Nor should you be the same nor would you want to."

— Elisabeth Kubler-Ross

G rief is not linear or a step-by-step process you will go through. It is a cycle and can start and stop, only to start again without warning. Later in the book, we discuss "Complicated Grief", but these diagnoses need to come from a licensed therapist. So do not let someone diagnose you, from the "cheap seats". Some of the worst pep talks I have heard, are centered around people trying to "Get you to snap out of it".

You will move through the grieving process at your own pace. In this book, we show you ways to help yourself in this unwanted journey. And also how to help your friends and loved ones understand and support you.

Just as grief has no time limit, neither does love. Love, as evidenced by our grief, does not end with death.

"To live in hearts we leave behind is not to die."

- Thomas Campbell

Stages... Really?

"The five stages of grief were never meant to tuck messy emotions into neat packages".

Elisabeth Kubler-Ross

Those who have served in the military deal with grief differently than those who haven't. Men and women grieve in different ways. Children show grief in a different way than adults do.

According to research, well over half of the people grieving the death of a loved one recover relatively quickly. However, 25% may take several years or longer to bounce back. 10% end up having what's called "complicated grief," a persistent, debilitating yearning. Complicated grief can hang on for years. Doctors and counselors used to believe that grief always proceeded in the same logical pattern. Current research reveals that this is simply not the case. However, the word has not yet spread to the masses, and people think this logical pattern is still science. Therefore, many believe that because they're not grieving according to this "logical pattern," known as The Five Stages of Grief, they're grieving wrong, and they start questioning themselves. They don't realize there is no right or wrong way to grieve. Each of us can and will grieve in our own way.

Where Did "The Five Stages of Grief" Come From?

You'll be surprised to know that the five stages of grief, as we know them, were introduced by Elisabeth Kubler-Ross in 1969 in a book titled On Death and Dying. For this book, she had interviewed several patients on their deathbeds about their experiences with their journey after learning they were dying. These five stages were intended to describe the emotional process of a person who was knowingly nearing the end of their life. There are major differences between what we might experience when we learn of our own impending death versus losing another person in our lives.

In 2004, Kubler-Ross and Kessler published the co-authored book, On Grief and Grieving. This book formally adapted these previously used five stages to the bereaved. However, the authors included a notice on the first page, which most people often ignore. Due to this ignored notice, the five stages are often misunderstood and incorrectly applied to grief in general. The ignored notice explains that the five stages are merely tools to help those grieving frame and identify their feelings. It goes on to say that they are "not stops on some linear timeline." It also explains that every person does not go through each stage and that those who do may not go through the stages in the order they are listed.

That being said, let's explore Kubler-Ross's Five Stages of Grief.

The Five Stages

As stated, these stages are not a pattern to be adhered to. They are merely a tool to help you understand and express your feelings to yourself and others.

Stage One: Denial

Denial is said to be the first stage of grief. The stage of "denial" is self-explanatory. In this stage, you pretty much deny that this thing causing you suffering has come to pass as you are overtaken with a state of shock.

According to Kubler-Ross, this stage helps you to survive the loss. You are numb. Life has become otherwise overwhelming and meaningless. We may deny that this thing that is causing so much grief has happened. This allows you to pretend that the circumstances do not exist. Denial is your mind's attempt to survive without facing reality. After all, if you accept reality, the overwhelming grief makes life unbearable.

But then you begin to accept reality. The denial begins to fade, allowing you to handle your grief a little bit at a time. This is the grace of denial. It enables you to cope with the feelings that begin to surface as denial begins to fade little by little. And little by little, you begin to accept.

The problem is that when you were denying that this horrible thing has happened, you were also delaying the inevitable emotions that come along with the grief. Now, as the denial fades, all those feelings begin to surface, and you enter other stages of grief.

Stage Two: Anger

Most people feel anger as part of the healing process. However, remember that not everyone feels every stage of the five stages of grief. Many people feel anger at other people — perhaps someone who didn't attend the funeral, someone who has changed since their loved one's death, someone who doesn't seem affected, or someone they may blame. Maybe they are angry at themselves for something they did or didn't do while their friend or family member was alive. Or perhaps they are mad at God.

Their anger may be expressed, or it may be suppressed anger they hold inside and let quietly seethe under the surface. Anger is an emotion most people fear feeling. We are afraid of what we'll do if we acknowledge our rage. However, Kubler-Ross believed that we must let ourselves feel this anger if we are going to heal. She taught that if we feel this anger, only then will it dissipate.

One day, as I talked to my wife, she admitted that she sometimes gets angry out of the blue. Our grandchildren, our surviving son, and I all experience the same emotion for no reason other than this is what grieving people sometimes do.

Stage Three: Bargaining

After someone dies, you may find yourself wishing against all odds that they were still with you. You may be having the "if only's.":

- "If only cancer had been found sooner..."
- "If only I had been with her on that hike..."
- "If only I had woken up in the middle of the night and in time to find him not breathing and resuscitate him...."

Then you may begin to bargain with God, "I will do anything; please just let me wake up, and this be a horrible nightmare." This "stage," as the other "stages," are not steps that you travel through. They are not set on a timeline. You do not enter a stage and exit it to enter another. As with the others, this stage may be entered for only minutes to be entered again later. You may find you cycle through the stages at your own pace, only to revisit some stages several times.

Stage Four: Depression

Another stage we may enter (and it's important to remember that these stages may not come in the order mentioned here) is depression. Once denial has worn off, we quit bargaining with God. At that moment, we are dropped squarely in the present. We are faced with the cold hard fact that we are living without our loved ones. There is an empty spot in our lives where they used to be. Our grief deepens, and we enter a new stage, a darkness that feels like it reaches our soul. It surrounds us and feels like it will pull us further into the pit of despair, never letting us go. We withdraw from everything and everyone we love. We fail to find pleasure in anything we used to find joy in. Nothing seems to make us smile anymore. And if we do smile, it seems shallow and empty. But the loss of our loved one weighs so heavily on our hearts that we simply cannot draw ourselves out of this bottomless, dark pit that we have found ourselves in. We have realized that they are gone, and they are not coming back. This is a normal step in your grief. It is not a sign of mental illness. You will overcome this depression.

Stage Five: Acceptance

The last stage of grief is acceptance. This stage is not being "okay" with the death of your loved one. This stage is about accepting reality. Your loved one has passed on, and you must live with that. No amount of bargaining or denial will change that.

Things have changed. Life will go on without them. You cannot keep everything as it was before they passed. You must accept that they have gone on.

You may build new relationships. You are not betraying the one you have lost. Life moves on.

You may still journey through stages of anger, depression, denial, and bargaining, but for the most part, you have accepted that this is the way that life will be from now on. You are not perfect. You will not be until you reach Heaven.

You cannot, however, reach this stage until you give grief its time. As I said in the beginning, it is amazing how quickly some people pass through the stages of grief. Others may take years. Your journey is individual to you. Don't feel like you must take a certain amount of time to grieve. Don't let anyone force you to move too quickly or take any longer than you feel necessary. Move at your own pace.

The "how, when, and where" of the stages of grief you experience really doesn't matter. You may not even experience each stage. That's OK. Rest assured; you are not grieving the wrong way. There is no right or wrong way to grieve.

Could there be A Sixth Stage?

David Kessler, who co-authored the book, On Grief and Grieving, with Elisabeth Kubler-Ross, added a sixth stage to the list— "Meaning." He came to understand this sixth stage better after the death of his son at the age of 21. He realized that "we are not a generation that is just okay with finding acceptance. We want to transform our grief into something more meaningful."

The stage of "Meaning" is merely the stage where we are looking and finding meaning in our loved one's death. I know of someone who can accept the fact of her miscarriage simply because she would not have her beautiful 15-year-old daughter if she had not lost her baby. She found meaning in her baby's death. Others have started non-profit foundations for children to fund research for SIDS, specific rare diseases, and other elements to help find meaning in their child's death. Whatever you choose to believe about these stages of grief, just know that according to Elisabeth Kubler-Ross herself, these stages of grief were "never meant to help tuck messy emotions into neat packages." Remember that they were merely meant as a guide to our emotions as we grieve.

So, How Do We Cope?

"It's so curious; One can resist tears and
'behave' very well in the hardest hours of
grief. But then someone makes you a
friendly sign behind a window, or one
notices that a flower that was in bud only
yesterday has suddenly blossomed, or a
letter slips from a drawer... and everything
collapses."

- Colette

Death happens. The Bible says, "It is appointed unto man once to die...." As such, grief is sure to come. Whether or not you are a believer, this truth is self-evident. The purpose of this book is not to win you to Christ. Our intention is to give you some comfort, understanding, and hope during what is undoubtedly one of the most difficult times you will face in your life. Therefore, it would be nothing short of foolish not to mention that God has given us ways to help us cope with the pain of loss, live through our grief, and put our life back together. It would be well worth your time to see what God has to say through the Bible or even Christian counseling. After all, what do you have to lose other than a little of your time which may be passing excruciatingly slow for you right now anyway?

As is the first step in any process, you must acknowledge that you have a need. In this case, the need is to survive the pain. Thankfully, God said that He "heals the brokenhearted" if we turn to Him. I do not know what I would do without God as my strength. Grief is so hard with Him to help me. I can only imagine what it is like for those who must endure it without His help.

Next, you must understand and accept that grief can bring on any number of unexpected emotions at any time—fear, peace, confusion, anger, guilt, joy, and so much more. You may be walking through the store and see something that reminds you that your father's birthday is just around the corner and begin bawling in front of everyone. You may suddenly get angry in the middle of pumping gasoline as you think how your daughter will never get the chance to pump gas into her first car.

These painful mental gymnastics always end in the same way. No answers. Just questions and painful emotions.

Maybe this happens to you too. Perhaps it doesn't. Nonetheless, expect feelings to surface unexpectedly at different times and for various reasons.

Never underestimate the value of seeking help in the grieving process. It may be difficult for you to reach out but getting support from other people who have been there or from people you know who care is invaluable. These can be friends or family members. This might be a support group or a counselor. In any case, it can help. Remember that no two people grieve alike; your grieving process will be individual to you. You are not strange or "different" because your grief does not look like others.

Plan for triggers. Holidays and birthdays are significant for many people. When those days come, know that it will be difficult, and plan for that. Plan a way to celebrate your loved one on those occasions. Anything you can do to make the day a little easier would-be effort well spent. Remind your family that the day maybe a little more difficult for you so that they know what to expect.

Often the most helpful thing you can do for yourself may seem counterintuitive. There is a tried-and-true way to put your own suffering at least momentarily in the background thereby reducing its severity. This "method' is to think of or do for others. Once again, it doesn't sound right. After all, your suffering is all about you-not others!

As an example, the author lost his first-born child and was facing the burden of a funeral the following day when he decided at the depth of his grief to visit another individual who was near death with cancer. That brief visit was a true respite from my own suffering.

Draw comfort from God. If you are a person of faith, prayer, reading the Scripture, and singing the hymns can offer solace. Attending services and spending time with the people of God can bring you comfort.

If you're beginning to question your faith, this may be causing you feelings of guilt or shame. This may be adding confusion to the mix of your already grieving mind. Speak to your pastor. He won't judge you. He'll offer help so that you can get your faith settled. This will help you to feel better all around.

Make sure that you are taking care of yourself. You cannot care for your emotional well-being if you are neglecting your physical well-being.

Studies have shown that grief affects the physical body. The brain activity of those who are grieving is different. They have different hormone patterns and a higher risk of health issues, known as bereavement-related health problems. Those suffering grief are also susceptible to several physical symptoms, including:

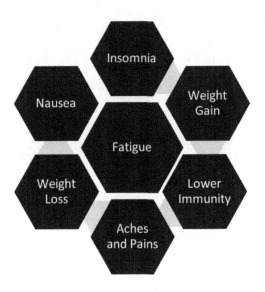

If you are experiencing any of these symptoms and want to minimize their impact, you must protect your health! Be sure to get enough sleep. Eat right. Watch your activity level. These things also play a part in how you feel psychologically and how well you deal with a traumatic experience, such as losing a loved one.

For some, it may be helpful to find a way to express yourself creatively. You might write a letter to your loved one, telling them everything you never had a chance to say before they passed, or journal about your feelings. Perhaps, you could put together a memory box or create a scrapbook to commemorate your loved one's life. If there was a cause important to your loved one, perhaps you could get involved in that cause or organization. There are so many things you could do in their memory!

Attempt to maintain your regular routine. Did you typically go for a run every evening or go to the gym in the afternoon? Keep that schedule. Did you go for coffee in the mornings and sit at the corner table for privacy? Keep doing that. Was your routine to go to bed at nine and read for an hour before falling asleep? Did you paint every Saturday or meet up with friends for dinner and a movie each weekend? There's a certain comfort in familiarity and routine. Plus, doing what you enjoy and connecting with those you love will help you cope and aid in your grief journey.

Lastly, you must learn to recognize the difference between genuine grief and clinical or significant depression. The stage of depression caused by grief is one thing. Major depression is something else entirely. You may need counseling or medication to help escape the grasp of significant depression.

Signs of Complicated Grief

"You must live! Though every fiber of your being may scream "end this pain now for I can bear it no more" to curl up and die is to dishonor the one for whom you ache so much."

-Ron Skinner

As mentioned earlier, you never completely get over the grief of losing a loved one, but if it continues to remain so constant and severe that you can't resume your life, you might be suffering from "complicated grief."

When you have complicated grief, you grieve so thoroughly and intensely for your loved one that it becomes debilitating and impacts multiple areas of your life negatively.

Symptoms include:

• Intrusive images or thoughts of the person
• Intense longing for the person
• Denial of the loved one's passing
• Avoiding anything that reminds you of that person
• Searching for your loved one
• Imagining they are still alive
• Feeling life is meaningless or empty
• Extreme bitterness or anger over the death of your loved one

With counseling, you can overcome complicated grief, and you can go on to live through your grief.

Major, or Clinical, Depression

I t can often be challenging to differentiate between major depression and grief. Remember that depression is one of the stages of grief. However, major depression is something different altogether. Let's take a deeper look at depression.

Grief and depression share many of the same symptoms. However, even in the middle of grief, you still cycle out of your stage of depression and find joy. Grief is a mix of good feelings and bad. Depression, though, is a constant feeling of emptiness and despair. There is no cycling. There is no hope. The good is not mixed in. You may feel as though there is no light at the end of the tunnel.

Depression also comes with other symptoms that do not typically accompany grief alone. These are:

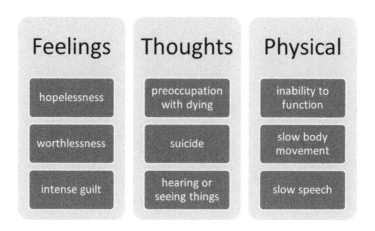

Feelings	Thoughts	Physical
hopelessness	preoccupation with dying	inability to function
worthlessness	suicide	slow body movement
intense guilt	hearing or seeing things	slow speech

When to Get Help

If you're experiencing any of the above symptoms of major depression, get help! There is no shame in talking to a mental health professional. If you are dealing with severe and persistent thoughts of self-harm, go to the emergency room, or call the suicide hotline. We have included helpful contact information in this book.

Failure to seek professional mental health care for complicated grief and depression may result in the development of significant emotional damage, life-threatening health problems, or suicide. Please don't be a statistic. Treatment can help you recover.

If you have any of the following symptoms, don't discount your symptoms either. Please contact a professional therapist or grief counselor if you:

- Are wishing you died too
- Feel as though it is not worth going on
- Have felt disconnected from other people for over two weeks
- Blame yourself for failing to stop your loved one from dying

- Blame yourself for your loved one's death
- Cannot perform your daily activities
- Cannot trust others as you used to before your loved one died

We all need help sometimes. Reach out when you need to!

Emergency Resources Nationally:

Dial 911

===========

Crisis Services:

24/7 Crisis Hotline: National Suicide Prevention Lifeline

Network

www.suicidepreventionlifeline.org

===========

National Suicide Lifeline:

(800) 273-TALK (8255) Veterans press 1

===========

Crisis Text Line:

Text TALK to 741-741 to text with a trained crisis counselor

from the Crisis Text Line for free, 24 / 7

===========

American Foundation for Suicide Prevention:

(800) 333-2377

===========

Veterans

send a text to 82825

===========

American Foundation for Suicide Prevention

www.afsp.org

What Coping Does Not Mean

Coping does not mean being "strong."

It's okay to feel sad or lonely. These are normal reactions. You are not weak if you cry. You don't need to be brave. Many people, feel like they need to protect their families by being "brave" in front of them. The truth is that showing emotions can help you and your family cope.

Remember when we talked about anger during the "stages" discussion? Some people get angry at those who do not express their emotions after the death of a loved one. Putting on a brave front could bring you into the uncomfortable situation of being the target of someone's unintentional anger as they pass through that stage of grief.

Secondly, coping does not always mean crying.

Wait! Didn't you just say coping meant expressing your emotions?

Yes. But there are other ways of expressing your emotions. Crying is a typical way to show sadness, but not everyone expresses sadness by crying. Some people express grief by keeping themselves busy. Others withdraw into their own world. Some get excitable, and still, others get irritable. Those who don't cry experience the pain of losing a loved one just as profoundly as those who do cry.

Coping does not mean experiencing all five stages of grief.

Kubler-Ross's five stages were named as five common experiences, not five required experiences. Elisabeth Kubler-Ross later regretted writing the stages the way she did. As she grew older, she noted that it saddened her that she did this because so many of her readers mistook the five stages of grief as being linear and as applying to every grieving individual.

Coping does not mean you are done grieving.

Just because you are coping well does not mean grieving has come to an end. There is no such thing as "closure" to death. You will still enter those stages of grief at times. You grieve because of the love you hold for the person you lost. That love will always be a part of you. That love will change, but it will never end.

You will find yourself living through your grief. Your grief is part of your love. Both are so much larger than any "stage." Kubler-Ross stated at the end of her life, "I am so much more than these five stages. And so are you."

Finding Your Way Now

"If you can't fly then run, if you can't run then walk, if you can't walk then crawl, but whatever you do you have to keep moving forward."

Martin Luther King Jr

Regardless of which stage of grief you're in, depending on your relationship to the one you lost, there may be a flood of responsibilities that you find pressed upon you. Responsibilities you're not ready to deal with. You must arrange for the services, body preparation, burial plots if they weren't prearranged, purchase the casket, figure out the finances now that your loved one has passed, and so much more! Financially, you must deal with the will and trust involved, distribute the remaining belongings, figure out how to pay for the funeral and how to live on one income, and deal with the life insurance company and other legal details. You may also be responsible for the well-being of children, or older children may be crowding around, and you may feel the need to be strong for them. All these responsibilities may be pressing in on you. What do you do first?

Recognize you are Grieving

First and foremost, give yourself a break! This is something utterly foreign to you. Though you may have lost other loved ones in the past, this time is so much harder! The path forward may not be clear to you. You are being and will be impacted by grief. Grief affects everyone and sometimes in ways that you do not expect.

You expect to cry. You expect to feel horrible. The truth is that some people feel relief, and some feel anger. There are many different reactions to grief.

Grief affects everyone differently and in many ways. It's an emotional reaction experienced on such a deep level that it can affect how you think, feel, and behave. It may even impact what you believe.

Common Grief Reactions

To attempt to list all the experiences your grief may bring would be an exercise in futility. You are unique. Needless to say, your experience with grief will also be uniquely yours. However, here are some reactions that we often experience. The following is not intended to be an all-inclusive list of what you might find yourself experiencing in the spiritual, cognitive, physical, emotional, and behavioral realms.

Physical Reactions

You may experience all or none of these reactions. For most of us, however, we will likely experience at least some of these reactions.

- Rapid Heartbeat
- Increased Blood Pressure
- Heaviness or Tightening in the Chest
- Exhaustion or Fatigue
- Feeling Weak or Faint
- Hollow Feeling in Stomach
- Muscle Tension, Pain, Achiness
- Hypersensitivity to Touch, Smell, Sights, and Sounds
- Headaches
- Deep Sighing
- Decreased Resistance to Illness
- Sleep Disturbances
- Weight Change

- Appetite Change
- Indigestion
- Sobbing
- Dry Mouth
- Lump in Throat

Spiritual Reactions

What has happened affects most of us on multiple levels of our life. Do not be surprised if you find yourself questioning things that you either never considered before or areas that you believed were settled in your life long ago.

Anger at God	Loss of Faith	Asking "Why?"
Changes in Values or Beliefs	Strengthening of Faith	Needing to Find Meaning in Loss

Emotional Reactions

The emotional component of grief probably comes as no surprise. What may catch us off guard is the severity and timing of some of those feelings. Much like a roller coaster, we don't know how high or low we may go. The twists and turns may be as unexpected as they are severe. Just hold on and know that you will make it.

- Despair
- Helplessness
- Hopelessness
- Depression
- Sadness

- Anger
- Feeling "Out of Control"
- Anxious
- Numbness
- Mood Swings
- Loneliness
- Yearning and Longing for the Loved One
- Guilt or Survivor Guilt
- Bitterness
- Calm
- Relief

Cognitive Reactions

Some of the cognitive effects of grief may be immediate. Disbelief and even confusion upon learning of your loved ones passing are very common. Other reactions such as struggling to concentrate, and memory loss may be very unexpected. The authors have experienced all these reactions at varying times. Some were fleeting, others we find we still intermittently experience years after our loss.

Cognitive Reactions
Disbelief
Searching to Understand
Difficulty Concentrating
Difficulty Making Simple Decisions
Short-Term Memory loss
Confusion
Decrease or Increase in Dreams
Preoccupation with Death or Loss
Suicidal Thoughts

Behavioral Reactions

It should not come as any surprise that our behavior may be affected to some degree. Anything that is so far-reaching in our life as to affect both the body and mind should be expected to affect our behavior as well.

Behavioral Reactions
Acting Out
Increase in Drug or Alcohol Use or the Misuse of Medications
Blaming Others
Avoidance of Situations or People
Decrease or Increase of Activity
Loss of Interest in Things we Once Enjoyed
Neglecting Ourselves

Don't forget that your Children are grieving too!

"You can often protect a child from the life's risks, but we cannot protect them from our sorrow-or their own. They simply have to endure it just as we must."

-Author Unknown

You must come to terms with your grief. If you have children in your home, they will need your love and support as well. Children cope well with losing a loved one when they have someone loving and patient with them. While this may seem so obvious as to not even need to be addressed, the reality is that we are often so absorbed with our own grief that we can sometimes neglect the needs of those closest to us. This time in your life requires that you be very attentive to your children's needs and give them time and attention.

One way to show concern and love for your child is to explain what is happening as much as you can before they start asking questions, then to listen to them calmly and patiently when they start asking questions. Be approachable! Don't just put on your happy face and tell them everything will be all right. They already know better. They are a part of this loss too. You do not want them to feel isolated in some misguided attempt to limit their pain. Talk to them and let them know that you are always there for them Children can't process what they don't understand, and they can't understand what they don't know. You might be thinking, "They are too young to understand fully. Therefore, they are too young to grieve." The truth is they recognize the changes. They need to understand the changes in their life. They will ask about them, and they will grieve in their own time and in their own way.

Don't try to dance around the subject. Be truthful. Use simple words your child can understand. Daddy's not coming back. Grandma has gone to Heaven. We'll see her again, but not until Jesus comes again or takes us to be with her. You'll never meet your baby brother because he's living with Jesus now.

Once again, remember that your child will grieve in their own time and in their own way. Remind your child that it's okay to grieve, but don't tell him how he should or shouldn't grieve. Just be there. Be the rock. Be the stability he needs. But be the comfort he craves.

We have talked briefly about the many things you may experience during this time. Still, we have not really touched on the seemingly endless practical tasks that need to be done. These tasks may now fall upon you. The world, after all, marches on even though it may seem to you that it shouldn't. This omission of the many details has been by design since we don't know where, on your grief journey, this book may find you. If your loss is very recent, such information may serve as a valuable reminder of what needs to be done. We have made available a downloadable pdf of "Things to Do" at the link below to help you track and plan. Remember that this is not an exhaustive list, and it may include items that don't pertain to you. It is just a practical guide and checklist, designed to help organize and remind you of things you may need to do.

If you are reading this book later in your journey, you may not need this resource. If, however, your loss is more recent, then you may find this to be a valuable source. If you know of someone suffering a loss please feel free to download and pass it along if you feel comfortable. The purpose of this book, after all, is to help as many grieving people as possible.

Use the QRC to access.

What About You?

"Grief is like the ocean; it comes on waves ebbing and flowing. Sometimes the water is calm, and sometimes it is overwhelming. All we can do is learn to swim."

Vicki Harrison

Finances, funeral arrangements, expenses, POA, closing accounts, insurance, bills—paying old ones and closing them out, and so much more all at the worst possible time... What about you? When and where do you grieve? As you have time, and sometimes your body and brain will just decide to make time whether you have it or not. That's the way grief works.

If you don't feel prepared, it's okay. No one does. If you're worried, join the crowd. We all are. Confused? That goes along with grief too. Perhaps you feel the need to act. Now, at least you know where to begin. Remember it is essential to take care of your health in the meantime—in the middle of the most trying time of your life. Grief is loaded with health-damaging effects. We know this. You know this. So, how can we minimize these effects?

Combating the Mind

Remember when we were talking about the effects of grief on the mind? A few things that will help you combat these are counseling and relaxing mind-body activities (meditation and yoga are two). Perhaps reading a good book is your preferred way of escape. The specifics of what may bring a temporary reprieve from the heaviness you are feeling is not important. What is essential is that you identify what works for you and do it.

Feeling overwhelmed with your grief, sorrow, and maybe even your future is expected. Find your place of escape and go there as often as you like.

Protecting Your Body

Getting a good night's sleep is vital to overcoming the emotional exhaustion of grief. Eating a well-balanced diet full of vegetables, lean proteins, and fruits will also help. Getting plenty of water is part of a healthy diet. A healthy diet also enables you to combat the physical elements of grief, including weight gain. Grief induces you to eat carb-heavy comfort foods. If you're filling up on healthy foods, you're less likely to eat many carb-heavy, fattening foods.

Another way to combat grief is to move your body. Even just getting out of the house and taking a simple walk can combat depression and agitation. Energy might be in low supply, but sometimes enlisting a workout buddy can make things so much simpler. It may feel counterintuitive but getting the body moving can actually increase your energy level and help your mood simultaneously. Do it whenever you can. Don't be too hard on yourself by setting unrealistic expectations but do try to stay moving. It will definitely help.

Remember that it can be easy to neglect yourself—your medications, your doctor visits, etc. These things are paramount to your health. Try setting the alarm on your phone to remind yourself to take your medicine. You might even ask a friend or family member to check with you every day to make sure you took them. There's nothing wrong with asking for help. You probably have people in your life that want to help but simply don't know what they can do. Reaching out for help can be a massive benefit to you in your time of grief.

What's more, it may also be allowing your family or friends to help in some way when they just don't know-how. You are now educating your family and friends on ways they can help and support you. Anytime you can help others while helping yourself is a Win-Win.

If you lost a spouse or other family member, you might now have new responsibilities on your shoulders. Some of those new responsibilities simply must be borne by you and you alone. There may be some areas that you find most stressful that would lend themselves well to reaching out to family and friends for help. Some discover that it is in keeping busy that they find the greatest escape from the pain of loss. Additional responsibilities can get your mind off your grief. The point is to embrace whatever works for you. Never let anyone, no matter how well-meaning, tell you that you aren't dealing with your loss well simply because they would have or perhaps did deal with their own loss differently. Keep in mind that we are referring to how you handle your loss, not whether you are functioning. If you have family or friends who see that you are not really living life or able to handle the day-to-day needs of your life, then listen to them and seek professional help.

And remember, when you're around people, you don't have to "have it all together." You're grieving, and they know you are. Allow yourself to grieve them fully. Right now, it's okay to feel like your life has fallen apart because it has. You will pick up the pieces and rebuild!

Outward Struggles of Grief

After everything else you've done, you've got more to do. These things will lead to outward struggles of grief. These outward struggles will invariably trigger inward struggles.

One of the times you'll most definitely struggle is while you're dealing with your loved one's clothes and other possessions.

How to Deal with Your Loved One's Possessions?

These wonderful things that once belonged to your loved one carry with them so many cherished memories. The scents that linger on his shirts. The perfume that sits on her nightstand. The teddy bear was going to be the first in his collection. What do you do with these? How do you deal with them?

At first, you may not want to part with them. They may bring comfort. They make you feel close to your loved one. Surely, they're still there. Surely, they haven't really passed on.

There may, however, come a day when those precious items begin to seem to represent more of a cloud over you when you see them. They begin to remind you that, yes, your loved one truly is gone. He's not coming back. They remind you with each glimpse that you're grieving his death.

You may be thinking of getting rid of the things. I mean, after all, someone else could use them, right?

But then the guilt hits. How could you even consider giving away her things? Isn't that like giving her away? I mean, who does that?

A crazy task, this job of dealing with your loved one's possessions. The great news is that there's no wrong way to go about it. It's up to you to decide when and how you will deal with your loved one's things. Don't let anyone tell you otherwise.

The disposition of a loved one's possessions can take on many forms. The variables that influence how their possessions are handled are almost endless. Still, a shortlist might include:

➢ What is your relationship to the deceased?

➢ Who is responsible for their affairs?

➢ Were they married?

➢ Did they rent their home or own their home?

➢ Were there children involved?

➢ How old was the one who passed? How old were the ones left behind?

➢ Personality—were they likable, and how will those who are left behind deal with loss?

➢ Financial position—was there insurance that would cover all expenses allowing those left behind to take their time in making decisions?

➢ Were the circumstances surrounding their death sudden and unexpected, or was it a slow lingering death that they knew was coming?

The above list barely scratches the surface of the variables at play.

The role that the keepsakes you have of your loved ones play in your life seems to change with time.

Dealing with the Family and Friends

It's not only the earthly goods he left behind, but your loved one's family and friends will remind you of him.

The same will be true for you. You'll find your loved one's family and friends to be each of these things—daily reminders, comfort, and pain. You must accept the bad with the good. Don't hide away from life. Get out there and face it. Accepting your loss is an essential part of what it takes to find joy in life once again.

Seeing Your Loved One in Unexpected Places

Places can trigger grief just as much as seeing a person or an object can. Traveling to a park your loved one used to visit often, walking past an ice cream shop, and remembering how they loved chocolate ice cream, or going to Walmart and seeing someone that resembles your loved one.

Reminders can be anywhere.

The Hurdles of Special Days

Anniversaries, birthdays, holidays... Each of these days can be difficult hurdles to clear each year. If your loved one died around a holiday or birthday, it could make it even harder.

Eric died on December 9th, 2013. Christmas was nearly nonexistent in our family that year.

We were pretty much numb that first Christmas. Even at that time, it was evident that this, the most cherished of all holidays, would never be the same for us again.

For many, Christmases as well as other special occasions may always have a dark cloud hanging over them.

Millions suffer each year as losses of a loved one have occurred around the same time as a special day in their life. These hurdles can reawaken grief years after your loved one's death and may last well beyond the holiday itself. This is called an "anniversary reaction." When you have an "anniversary reaction," you can experience intense emotions as though you just lost your loved one. These emotions include:

- Anxiety
- Guilt
- Trouble Sleeping
- Anger
- Crying Spells
- Depression

- Sadness
- Fatigue, or lack of energy
- Pain
- Loneliness

So.... What to Do?

Remember that it's normal to experience grief around the holidays, birthdays, and anniversaries. Be prepared for them. Planning a distraction to keep your mind off the time of the year instead of dwelling on it can be a great tactic.

Spend some time focusing on the great things about your relationship rather than the fact that they're no longer with you. Perhaps you might write them a letter or note about some of the great memories you have about them. You can add to this note every year.

Surround yourself with the people you love. Stay close to your support groups. Consider joining a grief support group.

Choose to start doing something special each year on that day. What is something that your loved one would have loved to have done? Would he have wanted to give to a charitable organization? Would she have wanted to plant a tree? Give or plant a tree every year in their name!

Lastly, let yourself grieve! It's okay to grieve. It's fine to feel sad. There's nothing wrong with anger, frustration, joy, depression, happiness, and everything that bounces in between. It's absolutely fine to cry and laugh—even at the same time! Do what you need, and don't worry what anyone else thinks.

If your grief becomes unbearable, gets worse with time rather than better, or interferes with your daily life, please see a mental health provider. They can help you.

Inward Struggles of Grief

We've talked about the outward struggles of grief, but what about the struggles that no one sees—the struggles that we battle secretly? Much of our identity may have been wrapped up in the loved one who died. Losses show up long after death in unexpected ways and at the worst possible times.

You're Suffering More Than One Loss

When you lose someone, you're not only suffering the loss of a loved one; you're losing so much more! A part of yourself has been ripped away. That person was part of who you were. They made you a parent, sibling, spouse, or grandparent, etc. Now, you no longer feel complete.

There's also a loss of security, especially if that loved one was a spouse or a parent. You feel shaken to the core. Your whole world is turned upside down. You relied on them. That is, to say the least, a significant loss.

Your family structure has changed. Perhaps the loved one who passed was a sibling, and the birth order in your family is different as a result. Maybe you lost your spouse, and now, all of a sudden, you are in charge of the family.

There's financial security lost if the loved one contributed to the family's income. It creates a burden that will be felt.

You lose the future with your loved one. You had so many plans with them, so many dreams, and those are gone. They'll never be realized.

Perhaps your loved one was someone whom you always felt you could confide in. The loss of a confidant is huge and can, in and of itself, be earth-shattering.

Be patient with yourself. That unique place in your life that they may have held did not happen overnight. It took years to develop. Why would we think that such a loss would not be felt for years to come?

Struggles... and More Struggles

There are some specific struggles that we go through when we lose loved ones. Some people experience relief when their loved one dies. Some may blame themselves or others. Still, others resent their loved ones for leaving them behind. The various battles we may contend with are many. Let's talk about a few.

Feelings of Relief

The unspoken emotion of grief. Before we begin, let me make clear that feelings of relief are not in any way an indication that this is what you wanted. According to the dictionary, relief is "a feeling of reassurance and relaxation following release from anxiety or stress".

There are several times that these feelings of relief may surface. One instance is when you have been endlessly caring for someone. Feelings of relief after their death are expected. It is not that you wanted them to die. It's that you have been watching them decline every day. You have seen their mental and physical anguish and have felt the strain on your own psychological and physical well-being.

Caregiving—especially for months and years—is wearying. You've given up a large part of your life to care for your loved one. You served someone else hand and foot and catered to their needs. Duties were never-ending, and tensions were high compared to how you lived your life before you started caring for your loved one. Now that they have passed, these duties have ended. These tensions have ceased. You can pick up the things you once loved to do again and live your life for yourself. That's freeing. It's normal to feel a sense of relief.

You may also have feelings of relief when death has been prolonged, especially if your loved one has been in pain. It is normal to have feelings of relief that they are no longer in pain and that their suffering has ended. They are in a better place, a place where they can walk, talk, and do everything they want to do.

When you've been worrying about impending death for an extended period, and that time comes, it can cause feelings of relief. Perhaps your loved one has been hanging on for a long while with cancer. Maybe it was more tragic; perhaps your loved one was an addict or was mentally ill, and you were constantly worrying about their suicidal tendencies. Your feeling does not come out of relief that they have passed, but out of relief that the constant fear and anxiety are finally a thing of the past.

Yet another time, you may feel relief, maybe when you were in an abusive or unhealthy relationship. I am not talking about the sense of justice or relief that results from the death of an abuser when the trauma or abuse is so severe that it makes the victim fearful because the abuser is still alive. I am talking about controlling, unhealthy, and problematic marital relationships or parent/child relationships. In these relationships, you did not hate the person. You did not want them to die, but you do feel a sense of relief when they do because you wanted out of the relationship but didn't know how to get out. You didn't want it to end through death. You would never have chosen it to end that way, but it did, and the fact that it is over is a relief in its own way.

You may feel "bad" for having feelings of relief. You may feel like you have some dark secret that you must keep hidden at all costs. The truth is that relief is widespread when death follows a time of intense pain, worry, suffering, or fear. No one wants to see their loved one in anguish, and it's only human not to want them to live in prolonged pain.

People are often ashamed when experiencing this normal feeling of relief because they don't understand it. Many people don't understand that you can experience relief and sadness simultaneously. You can be relieved that your loved one is no longer in pain and still be sad that they passed. Yet, many feel guilty because they falsely believe that if they feel relief, they must not feel sad enough. This simply is not true. You can miss your loved ones profoundly and still feel relieved that they are no longer suffering.

The Blame Game

Another feeling we struggle with is guilt. We tend to play the blame game. We sometimes feel guilty for the death of our loved one— "If I'd only realized he was sick a few months earlier…." "If I'd have been a match to donate a kidney…." "If I'd been a better spouse…." "If I'd only done more…."

Guilt

Elisabeth Kubler-Ross said, "Guilt is perhaps the most painful companion of death."

The truth is, it's not your fault. There's nothing you could have done differently. Guilt is a feeling and feeling guilty doesn't make you guilty.

Remember those stages of grief? Guilt is normal. It is normal to blame yourself for a time. There is a reason for this; it gives us a sense of control. If we blame ourselves for our loved one's death, it provides us with a feeling of control. After all, if it was our fault, we could have controlled whether they died or not.

Even in the unlikely event that you could have somehow prolonged their life had you been somewhere or known something or acted in some way, we must come to the realization that we are all destined to die and that the how, when, and where is not within our control. Even our own death is not for us to decide.

Although it's a normal part of grieving, you must be careful not to let guilt consume you. A study noted in The International Journal of Psychology shows that guilt intensifies grief and causes or intensifies depression.

Regret

There is also the feeling of regret, which is closely associated with guilt. Regret is the feeling we get when we have the "If I had known he was going to die, I would've…." "I could've…." "I should've…" thoughts. Perhaps you wish you'd worked less and spent more quality time with your loved one. Maybe you wish you'd said "I love you" more often. These are feelings of regret and must not be confused with guilt. Nonetheless, they hurt and must be worked through.

So, how do you cope with guilt and regret? First, as with anything else, acknowledge that you have them.

Next, determine if you're dealing with guilt or regret. If it's regret, consider talking to someone about how you feel, writing a letter to your loved one to get everything off your heart, and then allowing yourself to let go.

If you're dealing with guilt, realize that they are just feelings, and feelings can and often lie to us. Think through your guilt and how irrational it truly is. Could you honestly be guilty of your loved one's death? Admit to yourself that you are, in fact, innocent.

If your guilt is, in fact, rational—if you are truly guilty, you still have to work through your guilt. You must not allow it to create more pain in your life. Learn from experience, figure out how you can use it to help others, and forgive yourself. Your loved one would. Imagine what they would tell you. Would they forgive you? How can you do any less?

If you indeed do find yourself guilty upon careful self-examination, then focus on ways to make amends. It may be too late to make it right with your loved one, but it's not too late to do something kind for someone else in their name.

Lastly, take stock of your entire relationship with the one who has died. This would include the good, the bad, and the indifferent in your relationship regarding how you treated one another. Relationships are seldom as cut and dried as our memories and emotions would have us to believe. Strive to remember the things that you did right. This also helps with regret. Are you regretting not having spent more time with your loved one? Think about the time you did spend with her. Are you grieving the words you said in anger the day before he passed? Think about all the times you said, "I love you," and all the times you snuggled and whispered sweet nothings to each other. Look at the big picture. Look at all you've done for your loved one. How much time have you foolishly spent thinking about that one moment when you think you messed up? Try to see your relationship with the proper perspective.

Misplaced Guilt and Self Punishment

Many people tend to punish themselves for the misplaced guilt they experience. Not only does it not help, but it adds suffering to an already bad situation.

What is misplaced guilt?

There is a big difference between genuine guilt and misplaced guilt. We all fall short and should feel guilt at times for mistakes or things we may have done or failed to do intentionally. It is hard to confront the guilt associated with our shortcomings, It is also one of the things that separates us from all other animals. Remorse and guilt is a gift that helps us to change course and do better next time. Don't let your guilt take up permanent residence. Except responsibility and then forgive yourself.

Misplaced guilt, on the other hand, is an irrational reaction in which we take responsibility and blame ourselves for something, be it an event, or a loss, that was out of our control. Misplaced guilt is a common reaction when we experience trauma in our lives. When we consider that nothing is any more traumatic than losing a loved one it should come as no surprise that many of us struggle with misplaced guilt.

Remember that misplaced guilt is irrational. There are very few losses we experience in which your imagination can not conjure up ways that make it "your fault".

Examples of Misplaced Guilt

Maybe you bought the tickets for your loved one and the car accident on the way to the game that took their life never would have occurred had you not bought those tickets!

If only you had "made" him stop smoking he wouldn't have died of cancer.

"I should have noticed she was acting differently. If I had insisted, she see a doctor sooner..."

The scenarios are endless.

Why Do We Inflict Self-Punishment?

We often inflict self-punishment for one of the following three reasons:

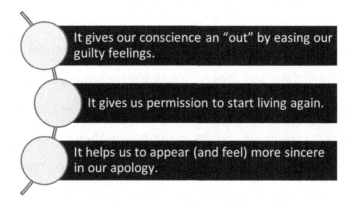

It gives our conscience an "out" by easing our guilty feelings.

It gives us permission to start living again.

It helps us to appear (and feel) more sincere in our apology.

But what if the guilt is misplaced? What if the guilt is irrational?

Guilt generally focuses on what you felt, did, or thought. No matter how misplaced it may be, guilt can get a hold on you that can become so severe that you find yourself willing to do anything to lessen its hold. This can, in some cases, even involve self-punishment in a misguided attempt to pay for your wrongdoing. This is not only irrational but destructive.

So... How do we overcome our Misplaced Guilt?

To heal, you must quit practicing self-punishment. To do this, you must first realize that you are dealing with this emotion.

Secondly, recognize your guilt as an honest and valid emotion. Guilt is a normal stage of grief, even if it is typically misplaced. Regardless of whether you want to feel it or not, you are. It's a part of your daily struggle. Ignoring it doesn't mean it doesn't exist, and it certainly won't make it disappear. This brings us to our next point.

Thirdly, you must allow yourself to feel the emotion of guilt. This may seem taboo, but it's simply the truth of the matter. As with any emotion, you cannot heal from it if you don't allow yourself to feel it. Running from emotion is like running from a dog; it just chases you with more vigor.

Next, refuse to judge your thoughts or emotions as "bad." Instead, you must learn to merely observe your thoughts and feelings. Rather than tagging your emotion as "bad," simply note that you had a feeling and move on.

Lastly, and possibly the most important, practice self-compassion! Being compassionate toward yourself is so vital while you're grieving. You're going through a tough time. Give yourself the freedom to grieve. Treat yourself as you would a friend who is grieving. Be kind and mindful toward yourself and treat yourself with respect.

What is self-punishment?

The American Psychological Association defines self-punishment as the act of inflicting physical or psychological harm on yourself for what you believe are your misdeeds.

We may self-punish by:

Refusing to be happy after a loss because you know deep down inside that you should "pay" for what has happened. You don't believe you deserve to be happy.

Intentionally sabotaging relationships so that you suffer as you think you should.

Subconsciously refusing to experience anything good in your life whether it be as important as a fulfilling relationship or as simple as hearing the birds chirping or noticing that the flowers are in bloom.

Self-punishment can be so subtle that it can be difficult to detect.

Remember that self-punishment is never healthy. It is always destructive. We can never right a wrong by inflicting another wrong, even if it is upon ourselves.

The Struggle of Resentment

Remember that the stages of grief often come at us with no rhyme or reason. They do not come in any specific order or for any specific amount of time. However, it is not uncommon for us to first experience the stage of denial before moving into anger.

This anger can manifest itself in many ways and in several directions. Some people get angry at themselves. Others get mad at the caretakers or doctors. Yet others find themselves angry at their loved ones for leaving them behind.

If we stay angry, if we don't face this emotion and work through it, it can turn into something deeper and darker. You may begin to resent the person who is the object of your anger, whether that be medical professionals, your loved one, or even yourself.

This resentment, if not dealt with, can settle in for the long haul, lasting ten, twenty, and thirty years. Some carry it to their grave.

Some people don't know what to do with their resentment. It causes more grief, so they try to numb it with alcohol, drugs, electronics, or emotional eating. This is where many addictions begin.

How Do I Win This Battle?

You know that your resentment was caused by your grief. Who do you resent, and why?

Next, you must create value around or in that person. Each time you find yourself resenting that person, change your thoughts. Think good thoughts, uplifting thoughts about that person instead. Think about why they are valuable. Why are they worthy of appreciation? Think about those things. You steer yourself away from resentment by training your brain to think good thoughts about this person rather than bad thoughts. Do not be fooled into believing you are somehow giving that person an underserved gift with such thinking. Ultimately, you will benefit the most by conquering this resentment you harbor towards that person.

Thinking good thoughts isn't enough. What can you do for the person to make them feel appreciated? Can you write them a note? Can you send them a text?

If you are the object of your resentment, can you do something for yourself? Can you take the time to read a book? Can you paint your nails? Can you promise yourself the time to go fishing with the guys this weekend?

If you find that you resent your loved one, can you do something in their honor? Can you volunteer at an animal shelter or a soup kitchen in their honor? Can you spend an hour with an elderly stranger in a nursing home? Can you write a note to them in your journal? Do something that places value on them.

When Resentment Rears its ugly Head yet Again

Even when it seems you won the battle against this struggle with resentment, it can rear its ugly head unexpectedly. You may be walking through the park, see a married couple happily sharing a moment together, and suddenly feel that dangerous emotion rears its ugly head yet again. It's not the end of the world. You know how to battle it. You know what to do. Don't succumb to its destructive outcome. You deserve far better than that!

Tears and Strength

"...we are all sorry when loss comes for us. The test of our character comes not in how many tears we shed but in how we act after those tears have dried"

— Michelle Moran

"You're so strong." You may have heard this, but what does it mean? Perhaps that person believes they would respond to the same grief that you're seemingly "making it through" by falling apart at the seams. But they don't see you at home when you can grieve—the tears that won't stop as they mingle with the shower water gently falling on your face. They don't understand that you must hold it together in front of your children. You must "be strong" for everyone else or merely for your own sanity. They don't know that you guard your emotions so carefully because if you were to begin crying, you might not be able to stop. Somehow, their comments, which are intended to be encouraging compliments, can have the unintended consequence of leaving you feeling misunderstood. Even worse, you may feel rage and an ever greater need to be "strong" for others. Whatever thoughts and emotions their words might stir, just remember they are only words. Let them go and move on.

Perhaps you find yourself on the other end of the spectrum when it comes to outward expressions of your emotions. Some people want to cry but find they cannot, regardless of how they try. This may make them feel like there is something wrong with them—like they are somehow not grieving their loved ones enough. However, as we have stated before, people grieve in different ways. Let your grief unfold the way it needs to and when it needs to. You cannot force a genuine reaction anyway. Don't try.

Isolation and Loneliness

"We bereaved are not alone. We belong to the largest company in all the world — the company of those who have known suffering"

– Helen Keller

While some people are clingy and need people, many people experience some degree of isolation after loss. If you are isolating yourself, know that this is not uncommon, nor is feeling lonely—even when surrounded by others.

There are several reasons for this. One is that the people around you are moving on with their lives as if nothing happened. For them, nothing did. They weren't affected as deeply as you were. It's not unusual for you to feel misunderstood, left out, cut off, and alienated from family and friends.

Many people experience mistrust, sadness, helplessness, anger, depression, and anxiety as they struggle with loss.

These things can lead to a desire to be alone.

Your tendency to disengage from those around you may be caused by so many different scenarios that an exhaustive list would be nearly impossible. Some of the more common reasons, however, might be:

- The usual, everyday things seem unimportant to you.
- Your loved one who passed was your closest friend.
- Those around you don't know what to say or how to act, which makes everyone uncomfortable.
- You feel as though those around you aren't tolerant of your grief.
- You simply don't care.
- You're scared of getting emotional in front of other people.
- You feel like you constantly have to console everyone else.

For many people, this phase will come and go. However, some people will find that their self-imposed isolation takes on a life of its own and becomes a destructive force to them.

Understanding Isolation

There are two types of isolation. These are Social Isolation and Emotional Isolation. We do not want to confuse either of these with mere loneliness, which goes hand-in-hand with grief. However, loneliness can also harm our emotional and spiritual state. We need to distinguish one from the other.

Social Isolation

Social isolation isn't just physically isolating yourself. It also has to do with psychologically distancing yourself from others.

Don't confuse this with being introverted. Those who are naturally introverted find alone time is vital to their well-being. However, when you no longer profit emotionally from the distance you've placed between yourself and others, then it becomes a problem.

Emotional Isolation

The last type of isolation is emotional isolation. When a person has been hurt by past relationships, they tend to put up walls that do not allow others in lest they get hurt again. This is emotional isolation. Perhaps they are withdrawing against betrayal, guilt, shame, stress, or pressure. They learn to keep their feelings to themselves and become completely despondent when sharing their emotions with their family and friends, keeping all their relationships on a superficial level.

How does this relate to those who are grieving? Sometimes, we may not feel as though we are being accepted or tolerated in our grief. People may respond in a way that we feel minimizes our grief, makes us feel uncomfortable expressing it, or makes us feel like we must move on. In this case, we may refuse to express our emotions to those around us and cut ourselves off emotionally from other people.

Loneliness

Loneliness is what we feel when we're not getting the amount or quality of social interaction that we want or believe we need. We feel unfulfilled in our relationships. Loneliness is relative. We can be in a crowd of people and be lonely because we're not bonding or relating in the way we need to.

The Risks of Loneliness and Isolation from Others

Loneliness and isolation can both affect you physically and mentally. As a psychological side effect, you can begin to have negative thoughts toward yourself. "I'm different. I don't fit in." You may also start to have negative thoughts about those around you. "They're all fake. All they do is lie." Or you may begin to have illogical thoughts. "They're talking about me. They don't like me." These thoughts may drive you to isolate further.

Loneliness and isolation also come with serious health risks such as increased blood pressure, hardening of the arteries, memory problems, inflammation, lower immune system, sleep problems, premature aging, and more!

Combating Loneliness and Isolation

If you find yourself starting to self-isolate, you should actively try to combat that. Here are a few ways to connect to others:

- Try a support group.
- Try group therapy.
- Go to a public place, like the park or some other social setting.
- Look for evidence that you are not alone.
- Accept an invitation to spend time with someone.
- Make eye contact or smile at others when going on a walk.
- Communicate by Facebook message, email, letter, text, or phone to a friend or family member.
- Ask people about themselves.
- Refuse to buy into the stories you're telling yourself and replace them with the truth.
- Volunteer somewhere where you'll have to interact with others.
- Look for similarities you share with others.

Overcoming

Combating loneliness and isolation is only one step in keeping your head up throughout your journey through grief. Though grieving is an inevitable part of life itself, you must be careful not to allow yourself to be overcome with these inward struggles of grief. Taking care of yourself is first and foremost in your struggle to survive and thrive through your grief. The following is a brief list of things that may help you on your journey through grief:

- Exercise regularly.
- Sleep at least seven hours every night.
- Join a support group.
- Spend time with friends or family who can offer support.
- Do things you love.
- Explore new skills.

If you find that you are unable or simply can't muster the strength or courage to take care of yourself, you must seek help from professionals. Remember that you are not alone in your struggle with this monster called grief, and sometimes we just need help. If some or all of the following seem to be persistent in your life for far too long, then seek professional help.

- Find it difficult to perform everyday activities
- Feel as though life holds no purpose
- Blame yourself or feel guilty for your loved one's death
- Have no desire to engage socially
- Wish that you had died along with your loved one

- Feel as though your life is no longer worth living

The "Suck it up and get over it" attitude so prevalent in our society can often be the wrong advice at the wrong time and may even be harmful. Such an attitude implies that you are weak if you feel too deeply or for too long. On the contrary, the courage to love so deeply that you feel as though you cannot go on after losing someone shows the strength of character. This, without a doubt, represents the best part of our humanity. It is NOT a weakness to seek help from others when needed.

If you have thoughts of harming yourself or of suicide, call the National Suicide Prevention Hotline at 800-273-8255, have someone take you to the hospital, or call 911.

The Fallacy of Closure

"Death ends a life, not a relationship"

– Mitch Albom

What Is Closure?

Closure, as defined by the Cambridge Dictionary, is "the feeling or act of bringing an unpleasant situation, time, or experience to an end, so that you can start new activities." Therefore, closure implies that there will come a day when you can wrap up all your grief, regret, sorrow, and never-ending loss in one neat little package, place it in a safe place, and never experience it again. Doesn't this sound like a great thing?

Our Uneasy Truce with Grief

Unfortunately, closure in grief, as most of us understand it, just isn't natural. Why is this so misunderstood?

Most people think of grief as being on a timeline, having a beginning and an end, when, in truth, grief has no end. Instead, it seems to go dormant at times to come out of the shadows and lay hold of you down the road at unforeseen times.

Grief follows no rules at all. Some people who believe grief passes through stages have the misconception that the stages are linear. They have the faulty perception that these stages happen in sequential order. As each stage is checked off, we move onto the next stage, moving on in our grief journey to never revisit that stage again. After all, we've conquered it, right? Wrong!

We have been led to believe the passage of time will provide closure and heal grief. This is another misconception. Grief never ends. That's the bad news. The good news is your grief will become less overwhelming with the passage of time. Life can and will be good again

We understandably equate grief with pain and suffering. Therefore, the words "Grief never ends" sound like "the pain never ends" to us, and the idea of living with unending pain is unimaginable.

The truth is that the ache of loss never really goes away... but you do learn to live through it. You keep loving that person. You keep missing that person. You may never stop seeing things that you used to do together and wishing they were there. You may never stop feeling that pang when their birthday rolls around. Though it does get more manageable, and though the times come fewer and further in between, there will always be times that you find yourself yearning for your loved one. As time passes, your grief may not be as raw on most days, yet on some days, it will be just as raw as the day you lost them. This is the reality of grief. But you do learn to live through it.

Expecting Closure is Inviting Disappointment

You've faced so many disappointments already—lost love, lost time, lost dreams, lost hopes, and so much more. You don't need anymore. You don't need anyone telling you that closure is possible. Expecting closure just brings long-term disappointment.

Closure may work in the business world, but such closure in the realm of grief is another thing altogether. We often expect "closure" to happen at different times in the process. We may expect the funeral to bring closure. Perhaps the day we go through our loved one's belongings will bring closure. Maybe closure will finally come with the first anniversary of our loss. Hoping some specific milestone will finally bring closure to your loss simply sets us up for disappointment.

You cannot lock the door on your emotions and throw away the key. If we genuinely did close the door on our emotions, detaching ourselves wholly from them, we would also be closing the door forever on the memory of our loved ones. To do that would be a worse loss.

"Healing" Without Closure

Since "closure" isn't possible, perhaps we should think, instead, in terms of healing. During the grief journey, we process our pain and begin to heal one level at a time.

Grief is like an onion. It's peeled back one layer at a time. With each layer comes more tears, but with each layer comes more healing. Each layer has its purpose.

As each layer of the onion is peeled away, it's used to make something beautiful. In the same sense, we learn to use our pain to help others and ourselves. In our healing, we can learn to breathe again, smile, and even love again.

Moving on in Your Grief

"Moving on" is a phrase we often hear in the world of grief and loss, but it's not very well understood, nor is it beneficial. If you ask any group of people what it means to "move on," what "moving on" looks like, or how to actually do it, you'll get a myriad of answers. Unfortunately, the answers to these questions are different for everyone, so I cannot be of much help either. However, there are a few things it is helpful to know about "moving on."

Moving On "In" Not Moving On "From"

Firstly, please realize that this section is about moving on "in" your grief, not moving on "from" your grief. You are grieving the past, the present, and what could have been in the future. That's a lot of grief. You don't move on from that. It touches you. It changes you. It becomes you.

However, you can move on in your grief journey. This lifelong journey is part of you now.

Others Do Not Define When You Move On

Those around you may be wanting you to "move on." You may believe they want you to stop grieving altogether—to stop crying, stop remembering, and stop hurting. You may think they want you to stop talking about your loss, to stop dwelling on the pain, and just accept life as it is. While it will not change how they feel or their reactions to your grief, it may be helpful for you to understand why they are responding to you the way they are.

The real reason they're asking you to "move on" is that your pain makes them feel uncomfortable. They love you. Therefore, they hurt because they see you hurting. However, that's not your fault, nor is it your battle to fight. You need to focus on yourself right now. You are not responsible for how they feel. You cannot change the way you feel, nor should you act differently in front of them because they cannot handle your grief. Don't let them dictate your grieving process, which is uniquely yours to endure. You need to let your grief unfold in the way that works for you.

You Define When You Will "Move On"

Again, everyone's grief is unique. Only you can define when you are ready to "move on" in your grief process. Don't let anyone push you. Each person moves forward at their own pace. Take your time. Let your grief be your own.

We Move on but Never Forget

Moving on in your grief is not about forgetting your loved one. Many people refuse to move on because they believe that to move on is to forget. Living through your grief is choosing to find some joy and purpose in life again. Emotions are not lineal nor exclusive. You can and will be both happy and sad- sometimes at the same time. You can eventually be glad you are alive and deeply sad that they are not. You can feel all of these things and more without betraying your loved one's memory. Sorrow and joy, beauty and loss coexist. You can embrace a full and happy life and still remember and honor the one you loved.

It Does Not Mean Grief Will End

As I said, grief does not end. Thus, "moving on" does not mean the end of grief. More so, it means moving forward in grief. It means getting stronger from the grief we carry. That "onion" gets smaller as we travel through the layers, taking up less space in our lives, but it never entirely disappears. It's there. It's a part of us now. Embrace it.

Does Time Heal all Wounds?

The last thing I want to point out about closure is that old and well-worn catchphrase that "time heals all wounds" is, to say the least, very misleading." Though it may be true, for the most part, that all physical wounds heal given enough time, even physical wounds, if severe enough, will leave a permanent scar that never goes away. Furthermore, depending on the severity of the wound, some injuries leave us forever changed. Sometimes these injuries may only leave physical scars. Other times there may be lifelong changes that only the injured experience.

Case in point, a few years back, the author experienced a very brief altercation with a handheld grinder. At that particular point in time, the grinder had a cutoff wheel installed. As a brief side note-human flesh and bone are no contest for a high rpm grinder with a cutoff wheel. Though I suffered a very deep gauge in my calf, given enough time, it has now healed, leaving only a deep scar on the surface attesting to my stupidity. The more significant damage has been to the nerves that were damaged deep in my leg. No matter the passage of time, this wound will never heal and has left a portion of my left leg with permanent nerve damage.

In many ways, injuries to the mind can share some similarities to physical injuries. In some less severe situations, the injury can be so minor as to heal completely without leaving a scar behind. Other times, such as the loss of a loved one or even a lifelong friend, there can be permanent scars that may forever alter who we are. When we lose someone, we love, it forever changes us. It defines who we are. It's a change in us that never goes back to the way it was. And that's a good thing. It makes us stronger.

So, no. Time doesn't heal all wounds, and there is no closure in grief. And that's okay. We'll get through this one step at a time and at our own pace. This is simply how it must be.

What Now?

The need for closure is part of human nature. We want to understand, and we want to understand right now! Without proper explanations, we find moving forward difficult. In fact, without these explanations, it's easy to spiral into depression. But the truth is that you don't always find all the answers. This makes closure impossible. So, what now?

Accept Your Emotions

Remember that grief is an unavoidable part of living. It's part of life itself. Remember that the stages of grief include many emotions and feelings—anger, sadness, denial, depression, bargaining, confusion, and more. Don't judge yourself for how you feel. Just let yourself feel it. When you suppress your feelings, you fail to heal. Furthermore, holding in your emotions leads to explosions (consider a balloon filled with too much air and ready to burst at any moment).

Focus on One Day at a Time

Take one step at a time, one day at a time. Focus on moving forward but do it slowly at first. Your grief will be fluid. Give yourself time. Plan one day at a time but do move forward.

Find Meaning in Your Life

Finding your purpose, especially if your purpose had been tied up in the lost loved one, can do great things in your healing process.

Perhaps you may find that your life takes on a new purpose—one that brings meaning to what your loved one went through. Many have started foundations because their loved ones fought certain diseases or conditions.

Maybe you'll find a new you entirely outside the role you played for your loved one. Life changes. So will you. These changes are not a betrayal but rather necessary growth in your life.

Talk to a Friend

You need someone to talk to, a confidant if you will, a shoulder to cry on. A good friend can offer a new perspective and advice. They can give you the support and love that's vital at this time in your life. A good friend is someone you can lean on in tough times. You may find that they can be not only a friend, but also a knight (or princess) in shining armor, and they're there to help you slay the dragon. Bring your friend onboard!

Be a Friend

Seeking to be a good friend to others seems counterintuitive at this point in your life. After all, you are the one who has suffered a loss so shouldn't it be all about you and your needs and no one else? The answer to that question is yes and no. Having your needs met is important. The secret that most of us seem to miss is that one of our greatest needs in life is to be needed by others! Every moment you spend thinking of or caring for a friend is a moment you cannot spend looking inward and focusing on your loss. It helps. Try it!

Talk to a Counselor or Grief Coach

When a friend just doesn't cut it, when the challenging times are just a little too challenging for the best dragon-slayer, it's time to turn to a counselor. Sometimes, you need the additional support that your friends may not be able to provide.

Grief counselors and grief coaches know what you're going through. They understand what you need and know how to help you through your most challenging times.

"The grieving process allows you to find a place for your loved one among the treasures of your heart. To grieve is to tenderly remember and feel that the time you shared with him or her was a great gift. It is understanding with all your heart that love doesn't end with death."

~ Jorge Bucay

Continuing the Race

"Well, everyone can master a grief but he
that has it"

— William Shakespeare

At some point, we must each come to a point where we realize that "Life must Go On!" Even if it is only a show at first, we will, we must, at least go through the motions. Eventually, going through the motions will transform into your new life's journey. A journey without your loved one. For some, this may be days, weeks, months, or even years after their loved one dies. For others, that reality may come crashing in upon them almost instantly. I am in awe of the way our mind works.

Though we may not understand at the time, our mind so often protects us from what is simply unbearable at the moment. Piece by piece, as you can endure the pain and sorrow, tiny fragments of painful reality will come to the surface.

It often seems to be more than we can stand as each piece of our new reality comes crashing in. There may be times when just that one realization will seem far more than you can bear. Imagine for a moment if every thought, every emotion, each new realization of what your loss has and will continue to cost you were to come in a single moment in time. I do not believe that our mind, or for that matter, our physical bodies, could survive such an onslaught.

Why We Disengage When We Grieve

Though the physical similarities in the death of our two sons were heartbreakingly similar as both died of self-inflicted gunshot wounds to the head, the way we processed those losses was different with each of our boys.

One of the hardest parts of all of this was realizing that life must go on without our sons. It's not "life as normal" anymore. It never will be.

We were tempted to disengage—from society, from tasks, from things we enjoyed, from everything. And we did at times. You probably will too.

Everyone has their days. You've committed to going out to a movie with friends. Still, it's been a long day, and "Oh! It would be so nice to just curl up with a good book under a warm blanket and just veg... alone. Besides," you argue, "it is raining." You're tired mentally and physically, and you just really don't feel like being with anyone. These are days we all face without grief added to the mix. You add in the element of grieving, and there are a whole new set of reasons for your withdrawal and disengagement from the world around you. Here are just a few:

- Your energy reserves are running on empty. You feel like you need to conserve the energy you have to deal with the emotional stresses that grief throws at you.
- You feel safer at home.
- You're worried you'll break down and start crying in public.
- You don't feel as though you can give 100% to any relationship or activity anyway.
- Social interaction scares you. After all, people ask that difficult question, "How are you?" and say stupid things that make you feel worse.
- You feel safer in your comfort zone of "not pushing yourself too hard."
- Doing "things" reminds you of your loved one.
- "Activities you once enjoyed" and "days out" just seem unimportant and not as fun anymore.
- "Doing things" without your loved one feels like a betrayal like you're "moving on."
- You feel incapable now or incompetent.

- You feel like you "just need more time," so you decide that staying home and "waiting it out" is the best way.

You fear the inevitable conversation of your friends as they discuss the lives of their children- a conversation that you simply can no longer participate in and don't even want to hear. It just hurts too much.

These feelings are normal to an extent. However, we must be very careful not to disengage for too long as it can contribute to depression. Depression, in turn, can cause you to isolate further, leading to more profound depression.

The most unfortunate thing is that when we travel the grief journey or battle depression, we may tend to shut others out. These are often the individuals who are most willing and able to help us in our time of need. We are, therefore, isolating ourselves from the very emotional and physical support we need most.

The things we often cut ourselves off from are the activities we used to enjoy. Perhaps we would enjoy them once more if we only tried.

Is this you? I'm not talking about life as you knew it before or going "back to normal" again. Try planning an activity that you used to enjoy doing with a friend or two and sticking to that plan. What's the worst that could happen?

Why Should We Engage?

Being social and engaging in activities we enjoy, whether those we used to enjoy or new activities, does several things for us regardless of what stage of life we're in, but especially when we're grieving. It gives us an outlet, providing us with a valuable way to cope with the emotions we're experiencing. It also gives us a chance to feel more fulfilled.

Some activities may offer other benefits as well. For instance, meditation may help you find peace and harmony. Perhaps a Yoga class could help you increase your physical well-being as well as get you back out with a few people. Art may help you feel satisfied or feel a sense of mastery. Activities may bring you closer to others, giving you closer relationships, which can be helpful. Any of these can help you feel better and feeling better even a little makes a big difference!

How Do We Engage?

We know that we need to engage but knowing what needs to be done and acting on that knowledge are two very different things. Sometimes, it's not that you don't want to "get back in the saddle" again, so to speak. Frequently, it's just the how-to part that makes it so hard. As with many things in life, the secret to succeeding is planning, implementing, and sticking to it.

Dig Deep

Before you can plan out your day, you need to know what your day consists of currently. That may seem so basic as to not be worth mentioning at all. After all, we all know what our days consist of-were living them each day! It is sometimes surprising how many of the truths we hold, upon self-examination, are not as they seem. The following exercise may seem silly to you at first. If you are willing to put forth the effort you might be surprised how helpful it can be.

Sit down with a daily schedule and write out everything you do hour-to-hour, the time you do it, and how long it takes. This way, you can easily see what's filling up your time.

After your hour-by-hour schedule is written down, really look at it. Are you doing too much? Too little? Determine if any of the activities on your list feel like a drain on you emotionally. Highlight these in red. What are things done out of avoidance or worry? Highlight these in pink. Highlight those activities that are centered around self-care, positivity, and coping in green. Finally, list the things you've cut out that used to be important to your day. Lay these lists side-by-side. How many productive things have you quit doing that were once important to you or your well-being? Why?

Decide on a Strategy

Now, it's time to plan. Which things in the red area need to be in your schedule, whether they drain you or not? Keep these and throw out the rest.

What can you cut out of your schedule from the pink area? Not only are they not helping you along on your grief journey, but perhaps they are making things worse. Be honest with yourself, and then cut out what you can from these items.

Everything in the green stays. What else can you add to your list that you used to do that would be highlighted green if listed? Give yourself some time to think about that, and then add it to your green list. You may find that once you start doing some of the activities you have been avoiding, you begin enjoying them again.

What Should be Part of Our Plan?

So how do you stick to your schedule in those tough times? How do you go on with life? How do you force yourself away from avoidance and into engagement with life? Much of this has to do with making sure the right things are in your plan.

We've already talked about adding in the things that will help you cope and manage your grief. We have also discussed cutting out the bad things that may be hindering your grief journey. But what other things can help you to manage your grief?

Exercise

One thing you should add to your schedule is exercise. Exercising helps you eat healthier. I know, I know, for many of us, the mere suggestion of exercise can have such negative connotations that we tend to simply pass by such a notion altogether. Still, exercise doesn't necessarily mean a grueling hour on that treadmill or a hundred pushups every morning. For the benefits, we are talking about, a leisurely walk in the morning or the cool of the evening is enough. Believe it or not, simply going for a daily walk can have a profound psychological impact. Over time, you might even find that you are reaping additional benefits, such as losing those few stubborn pounds in the process. This, in turn, may help you to feel better about yourself. As you feel better about yourself, you become more optimistic, less stressed, and more energetic. All of these things can help you in your grief journey. Again, this may sound counterintuitive as the last thing you really want is to get up and move since you have neither the inclination nor the energy. But that's just the point! Countless people can attest to the fact that getting moving boosts both your energy level and your attitude. I know it is not easy but do it anyway!

Grief Therapy or Grief Coaching

A grief therapist or grief coach can do quite a bit to help you. One way they help is by literally coaching you through your grief. They direct you in the steps you must take in your grief journey to make it through. They provide a strategy for overcoming the most challenging times and give you exercises (oops-sorry about that dirty word -exercise popping up so soon after the above paragraph) to help you learn and implement the strategy.

Another large part of grief therapy is getting the chance to talk through your grief. You may not feel like you can express the deepest parts of your grief to your friends or family or even to your spouse. Still, a grief therapist or grief coach gives you a safe place to vent and express your deepest emotions without feeling judged.

Group Counseling or Group Coaching

Another thing you may want to consider is group counseling or group coaching. Being among others who have also experienced loss and are traveling a similar journey can be helpful for some. They can understand what you're going through because they may be going through similar struggles themselves.

Another reason group coaching or group counseling helps is because while you're receiving help and comfort from others, you're also providing it. Helping others in their journey through grief gets your mind off of yourself and onto the good you can do in the world. The realization that you can help others because of what you've gone through is comforting in itself. Though not always widely practiced, it is well documented that focusing on others rather than yourself brings greater joy not only when we are sad but even when things are going well in our lives. Try it. You might be surprised.

Socializing

You've probably already considered adding this to your schedule. After all, it's one of those things that you've probably been avoiding. I know we did. We just wanted to be alone where we could grieve without judgment. However, being with friends will aid in your grief journey.

If you don't want to engage with your friends, join a grief support group and make some connections around your common goal, healing.

Set Goals

The last thing I will mention, and perhaps this should be at the top, is to set long-term and short-term goals. Goal setting is merely creating a plan for your days, weeks, and months. When you do this, it gives you a certain feeling of control over your life in a time when life may feel out of control.

Do It

Now that you know what you need to have in your schedule, it's time to build that schedule! Using a daily planner, literally schedule these things into your week. Make sure you're not trying to plan too much on one day. You don't want to discourage yourself by setting an unrealistic goal that you can't meet. Remember, they are your goals, and they can be changed at any time as you see fit.

Just having a schedule will make you feel better. Having good things in your schedule and kicking the bad out will further that. However, that doesn't mean that challenging times won't come. You will still experience painful emotions. You'll still deal with doubt, frustration, sorrow, discouragement, and many other emotions. Regardless, you must choose to stick to your schedule. Keep "doing" even if you don't feel like it. This is part of coping. You'll feel better about yourself if you do.

Engaging in a New Life

You might be wondering, "Ron, why do you say a new life?" You know the reality of the situation—the truth we don't want to face. Our loved ones are an intricate part of our life. They make up a significant part of our world. Regardless of the amount of space they took up in our world, our life will never be the same without them. We cannot return to life as it once was. It no longer exists. Therefore, we have one option: learning to function and even thrive in this new life without them.

What Will Change?

You may notice that several things change in your life with the death of someone dear to you. The following areas are in no way all-inclusive;

Your Activities

The first place you may notice a change is in your activities. You may lose interest in activities you once enjoyed. Perhaps you were participating in some things merely because your spouse enjoyed them. These may no longer hold interest for you. You may also develop new interests. Perhaps you'll start filling your empty time with volunteer work or become involved in a cause that was important to your loved one. Whatever the case may be for you, learn to enjoy these new facets of your life.

Your Employment and Finances

Another thing that may change is your employment status and finances. If your spouse worked, whether, inside the home or out, the odds are that you're going to have to fill in the gap in finances that is left. You may have to get a job or find a new job that pays more if you're currently working.

If your spouse stays at home with the children, finances will also change. You will suddenly need daycare or a babysitter while you work.

Your Faith

You might notice changes in your faith. Some people question their faith after the death of a loved one. Others grow stronger in their faith. Though it may not always seem to be the case, this significant change in life is an excellent opportunity to really examine what you believe to be true.

Your Priorities:

Your priorities may change. If you lost a child, your focus might become your other children or your spouse. While this may be a common occurrence with grief -no matter how you feel or what changes may occur as far as the focus of your life, you must choose to make your health a priority. This may be new for you. Parents, especially, have a difficult time setting themselves as a priority in their life. However, this is vital if you are going to work through this grief and come out stronger. Whoever it is that you have lost, I have to believe that if your love was so profound for them, they must surely have loved you much the same. It would be insulting to assume I could know what they would have wanted for you after their death. However, I will ask you to contemplate what they likely would have desired for you based on your relationship with them. Would they want you to take care of yourself physically, emotionally, and even financially in their absence? Would they have preferred you remain alone for the rest of your life rather than find new relationships?

Your Relationships

Be prepared for the possibility that some of your relationships may change. You may notice that some friends or family keep their distance. This is likely because they don't know what to say or how to say it. You may have couples you were close to that no longer feel that you fit together the same way without your spouse. Perhaps they just don't know how to adjust. Try not to harbor resentment towards them. Consider that you may also feel things have changed, and it is now not so natural to interact with them as it once was. You may also find that some friends and family members become closer than you could have imagined. You may drift from some friends and acquaintances when your priorities and activities shift, and you may gain new ones. If there are relationships you honestly would prefer to hang onto, even though things have changed, and it is difficult to talk to them in person, then send them a text, email, or letter to let them know how you feel. They may be all it takes to rebuild that relationship.

Your Responsibilities

Your responsibilities may change with the death of your loved one. This, of course, depends on who that loved one is to you and how much responsibility you held in their life. If you were the primary caregiver for a sickly family member, your responsibilities would shift quite a bit. That responsibility ended. You may feel lost, and you may not know what to do with yourself. I urge you to find productive activities to fill your time.

Your Routine

We like our routines. Studies have shown that even nightly routines before going to bed can help us feel calm and ready for sleep. What those routines consist of doesn't really seem to matter. It's simply through the completion of those routines that we derive benefit. Some of your routines will likely change, particularly if your loved one lives in your household. Many people live by routine, so if the death of your loved one brought about changes in your routine, you might feel a bit more unsettled than others. You may feel flustered. Your days may seem empty. This is entirely normal. Establishing new routines may bring unexpected benefits for you as you'll feel safer and more in control. Even routines can sometimes help to feel that there is purpose in our lives again. The more quickly you get settled into a set routine, the better.

How Do You Deal with Change?

Change can be difficult. Unfortunately, when we lose a loved one, we don't have the option of dismissing change from our life. It's coming whether we want it to or not. So, how do you deal with change?

Ask for Help. Many of us (especially men) can find asking for help a little complicated. We somehow see it as a failure, but it's far from that. Asking for help when you need it is one of the strongest things you can do—especially if your pride is getting in the way. If you need help but can't bring yourself to ask a friend or family member, hire someone to help you.

Another area you might need help is in learning those areas that are foreign to you. I know of an older woman whose husband passed. Suddenly, she was forced to learn to do something new; she had never pumped gasoline. She had to ask her son to teach her how. Others have never balanced a checkbook, never cleaned, or never ran a weed eater. Though these may seem like simple things to some of us, they are anything but simple if you've never learned how to do these things. Ask for help or take a class to learn. And please remember, once you find the courage to set aside your pride, it is very likely that you have family or friends that would be happy to help.

Accept Help

Our friends and family are there for us. They want to help you in any way they can. However, human beings tend to be set on helping themselves, whether they truly can or not. We'll deny that we need help until we turn blue in the face, all the while wishing that someone would just jump in and help despite our denial. Let others help you.

Perhaps you are having a difficult time accepting help with chores around the house. You may feel like it's your responsibility and that, "by God," you're going to do it or die trying. Many people face this dilemma. If you have children in the home, consider sharing the responsibilities. Even young children can be entrusted with a few household chores. The truth is that they see you struggling too. They want to help. They need to help. You need to let them. Feeling needed is as essential for them to as it is for you, so don't deprive them of being a part of the new normal in their lives.

Don't Make Big Decisions

Most professionals agree that big decisions should wait for at least a year after your loved one has passed. The first year is a very emotional time. Grief runs rampant, and you don't want to make a big decision based on your fragile emotional state.

If you must make a big decision, ponder it long and hard before making the leap. If you pray, be sure to bring it before God.

Another great thing to do is consider asking others for advice on the idea before deciding. This will help you see outside perspectives from those who may assess the situation more clearly.

Get Advice on Your Career

If you need to search for a job for the first time or for the first time in a long while, or if you need a new career that pays more, it may be time to ask for help, yet again. A career counselor can be of great help in this area. Not only do they help you choose the career you're best suited for, but they help you with your resume and help you to search for a job!

Many county and state governments have free career training available. They also typically have free career counseling services.

Get Help with Legal and Financial Areas

Did your parent or spouse have an estate that needs to be settled? Was there a will left behind? Do you need to revamp your own will? Are there financial issues that must be resolved? If your loved one left a large or complicated estate, then trying to handle these things on your own can seem overwhelming. Hiring a lawyer or financial specialist (i.e., financial advisor or accountant) can take a significant burden off your shoulders.

On the other hand, if their financial affairs were straightforward, you may choose to research and do what little needs to be done on your own. Prioritize and remember that very few things are so time-sensitive that they absolutely must be done today. Self-imposed deadlines in areas that are not time-sensitive may serve only to heighten your stress.

Keep a Journal

A journal isn't just for expressing your thoughts and emotions, though that is a great reason to keep one when you're grieving. It is also a good place to write down your priorities and plans. When you do, they feel more set in stone, and you're compelled to follow through. Just having one place to jot down every phone number you have called or may need to call and check off every "To Do" you have completed and recording additional items on your list makes having a journal well worthwhile. A little organization never hurts anyone, and, let's face it, your organizational skills may not be at peak performance right now.

Another reason for keeping a journal is for reference. Do you need some encouragement? Look back at your journal and see how far you've come in your grief journey! You change a lot with time. You grow. Seeing it will help you realize that there is light at the end of the tunnel, and you're headed in the right direction.

Stay Positive

Sometimes, making these changes and doing these new things may feel disloyal to your loved one. Nothing could be further from the truth. Setting new goals for the future and enjoying new things is a positive thing in your life.

Engaging with Others

Sometimes, the most challenging part can be engaging with other people. Some people may avoid the elephant in the room, not knowing how to act around you. Those who do say things to you misspeak or say something awkward. Try to understand that this is as new to them as it is to you. In all honesty, you have probably been in their shoes in the past.

- Their response to your loss is affected by several factors. A few of these factors are:
- Have they suffered a loss? How long ago, and who did they lose?
- What was their relationship to the person who you lost?
- What is the person's gender?
- How old are they?
- What is their personality?
- What are their life circumstances?
- And more.

People will say things to you that are just plain dumb or painful. They will not mean to. They'll think they're helping, and if you were exactly the same age, gender, personality and had the same life circumstances and thought process as they have, you might find it helpful too. However, you're not coming from the same perspective, so it's going to sound heartless or superficial.

People Sometimes say the Most Hurtful Things

"The whole world can become the enemy

when you lose what you love"

– Kristina McMorris

An entire book could be written about the dumb and hurtful things people sometimes say. I believe most people have the sincerest of intentions. Still, they either have no real reference point to understand your grief, or they will think of the most relevant loss they may have experienced in their own life and insinuate it is the same as your loss. Hence, they understand what you're going through. Of course, that is never really the case. I believe still others will speak out of nervousness or some misplaced obligation to give some helpful words of wisdom.

Two of the most egregious things that were said directly to us were as follows:

The first incident occurred after the loss of our first-born child. In this instance, a new acquaintance doing some work for us on a rental called about some detail (supplies he needed, as I recall). I explained it would likely be a week or so before I would be able to get the supplies he needed. I felt it only right to explain the reason for the delay, so I briefly explained that we had tragically just lost our oldest son. His response over the phone I will never forget," "Yeah, I know exactly what you are going through. My best friend's mother-in-law just died, and I had to go to the funeral."

The second time we were struck by the pain of another person's words as they attempted to empathize occurred as we were standing over the casket of our son Eric. We lost Eric about 16 months after the death of his older brother Adam. Needless to say, we were still very raw from the loss of our firstborn, who left behind two children. Now, we found ourselves standing over the casket of our fallen soldier. He left behind a wife and four children. When one young man's turn to approach us and pay his respects came, the following words flowed from his mouth: "Bummer man, you've lost two-but at least you still have one left."

It is likely that you, too, will suffer such things. Below is a very brief list of very common things that people may say to you.

- At least they're not suffering anymore.
- It wasn't meant to be.
- God is in charge.
- Everything happens for a reason.
- Time will heal this.
- You have to be strong for your children.
- They're together now.
- Others have it worse than you.
- You'll be okay after a while.
- You need to put this behind you.
- I'm surprised you're still so upset.
- He brought this on himself.
- She's been gone so long. Aren't you over it yet?
- You're lucky you had so long with him.
- At least you have more children.
- It was just a cat. You can get another.
- I know just how you feel.
- Just move on.
- You must be strong.
- Heaven needed another angel.
- You'll feel better if you {*Fill-in the blank.*}

Understand that, although they seem to be making things worse, they are genuinely trying to fix and minimize your grief. They don't realize the comments may be hurtful or offensive. They are trying to help.

How to Respond

When people do say the wrong thing, how should you respond? What do you say to the hurtful things?

Assume They Have The Best of Intentions.

It is likely that there was a moment in your own life when you orchestrated the classical "Open mouth, insert foot" maneuver yourself. Remember that most people do not mean to hurt you. On the contrary, they are trying to comfort you and "screwing it up". They love you or, at the very least, harbor no ill will towards you and don't want to see you sad and suffering like you are, so they're trying to help you see the silver lining. But they end up doing it in the wrong way. It can help you if you remember their intentions.

Tell Them How They Can Help

Your support system really does want to help, but they can't do that if you don't tell them how and where they can. Open up and share with them what you need.

Sometimes the need is for a little space. If you need people to quit stopping in so much, tell them.

Sometimes it means less talk about how your loved one died. Share that need.

Tell them how they can help. Typically, they'll be happy to oblige.

Use It as a Learning Experience

Lastly, rather than taking it to heart, take it as a learning experience of what not to do when it comes to your turn to comfort someone else. Rather than saying the above phrases, try these instead:

- I can't imagine
- We love you
- There are no words
- I'm sorry for your loss.
- I'm just a call away.
- I'm here to help in whatever way you need.
- Let's go get some coffee.
- I'm bringing over dinner.
- I wish I had the words to say. Just know I care.

These responses don't try to fix the unfixable. They don't try to tell those who have lost a loved one what to feel. Just remember to be caring, kind, and compassionate. Rather than getting angry at the comments of others, use this time as a learning experience of what to say and not say to others. Learning from our bad experiences makes those encounters worthwhile.

Specific Relational and Conditional Losses

The loss of a loved one differs depending on who that loved one was. It was different for me losing my sons than it would be for you to lose your spouse, grandparent, sibling, or father, etc. In fact, even if you lost your sons, your grief would still be uniquely your own.

In this chapter, we address losses based on some common relationships. Please note that the loss of a beloved pet can be felt just as deeply for some as the loss of another person for others. Grief is unique to everyone.

As a quick side note to the above, please remember that while you may have felt the loss of a beloved pet just as deeply as your best friend is feeling the loss of her husband does NOT mean that it is appropriate or helpful to make that comparison in an attempt to empathize. Once again, all grief is unique

The Loss of a Spouse

All loss is unique, but, in many ways, the loss of your lifemate is a particularly painful loss that affects nearly every moment of the rest of your life. Some experts say it thrusts a new identity upon you that takes years to adjust to.

Think of it this way; you're used to having someone around all the time. You come home from work, and they're there. You hear a joke and immediately tell it to them. You share everything with that person. Suddenly, they're gone from your life. To say that this is a significant loss would be to trivialize the depth of your loss and the ensuing grief you are enduring. It is your spouse that you find yourself reaching out to often throughout each day. You find yourself still setting the table for two or turning to tell them what you just read. You shared your entire life, your hopes, and dreams as well as your trials and triumphs. Though we love our children beyond measure, we always know that they will leave the home and live their own lives one day. This is normal. Our spouse, on the other hand, we expect will always be there for us. Still, the unimaginable horror of losing the one with whom you have built your life is thought so horrendous that we generally just don't give such a scenario the time of day.

Challenges

The two biggest challenges when losing a spouse are loneliness and finances. Your spouse was a daily part of your life. You acutely miss their presence and everything about them. You may feel lonely—even when you're around others because you're not with your spouse. You are not necessarily destined for a life of loneliness. Reach out to others for support. Don't isolate yourself, as tempting as it might be. Self-imposed loneliness is not the key.

Finances are another challenge with losing a spouse, whether they were the breadwinner or merely the one who managed the books. Whether they were the one who held the job, or you were a two-income household, there may be a gap that must be filled.

If your spouse handled the finances, then there may be a challenge there as well. There will be passwords to locate, books to figure, bills to manage, and more. Besides this, you'll have the funeral expenses and possibly hospital bills or hospice to figure out as well. It may be helpful to enlist a trusted family friend or family member to help.

How NOT to Handle the Loss of a Spouse

Let's talk about some of the misconceptions about handling grief when losing a spouse. These include the unspoken assumption that you must grieve alone, that you must "be strong" for others, and that you can or should replace the loss. These myths can be hurtful to you and those around you.

Grieve Alone

This isn't necessarily something that people tell you to do or something that we set out to do. It can happen by default as friends and family withdraw to go about their own lives. At other times, those who are grieving choose to isolate themselves as a form of self-protection. Grieving alone is one of the worst things you can do. It may be hard but for your own benefit, embrace those around you who care. Life is not complete when lived alone.

Be Strong for "*{fill-in the black}*."

People tell you to be strong for your children. This is hurtful. It not only denies you the ability to grieve, but it suggests that you are supposed to lie to them as well as the world.

"How are you today?"

"I'm fine."

What are you telling your children when you don't allow yourself to grieve? You tell them that it's not okay to grieve and that it's inappropriate to express your emotions. This is not the message you want to send.

Allow yourself to grieve your loss. Allow your children to see you grieve. Support each other. You need that. They need that.

Find Someone to Replace Your Loss.

There are several websites out there related to the possibility of replacing loss right away. Many people equate finding new love with happiness, but this simply is not the case.

Several years ago, a study found that an astonishing number of widows and widowers were remarried within 12 months of losing their spouses. However, this same study also found that many of those same marriages were experiencing severe issues or failing by the 2-year-mark.

We are not discouraging remarriage. Remarriage after loss does not equate to failure. However, remarriage simply to replace that which you lost may. Many people find companionship once again, but if you're going to remarry, make sure it's for the right reason—love. If you should choose to remarry, please know that there is no "right amount of time" to grieve.

Enduring Grief

So how do you handle the grief of losing your spouse? How do you travel this overwhelming, frightening, and sometimes lonely journey? For anyone to suggest that they know best how to handle your grief is both useless and hurtful. Not even you can know how to deal with this thing called grief. You will, by necessity, discover what works for you as you travel this long and winding road called grief. The below is simply some areas that many who have and are grieving have found helpful.

Grieve as Necessary

You lost a part of yourself—your other half. You lost your life companion. You may not be sure who you are without your spouse. This is normal. Many people find their spouse defines who they are. Losing them can be disorienting, to say the least. You need to grieve that loss.

You may feel like you need to be strong. You may feel as though grieving will make your loss too real. However, mourning your loss is an essential part of the grief journey. Let yourself grieve as necessary but always when and how you see fit.

Talk about Your Spouse

Talk to others about the love of your life. Talk about what you miss about him. Talk about his strength. Talk about her calmness. Tell others that you're lonely and why. Share about how your spouse died and how that makes you feel. Speaking from your heart will help you in the grief process. Remember that the right amount of discussion about your spouse is always exactly what you are comfortable with at the moment at hand. Period. It may be no discussion at all, or it may be hours on end.

Respect Your Limits

You'll have emotional and physical limits after the loss of your spouse. You'll probably be more tired than usual, and your energy level may be low. You may not be able to think as clearly. You'll be on an emotional roller coaster and be mentally and physically worn out. Respect your limits. Treat yourself like you'd treat a good friend. Don't trivialize what you're going through. Don't be too hard on yourself.

Remember that holidays, anniversaries, and birthdays may be especially tough. Be exceptionally compassionate with yourself during these times.

The Loss of a Child

Losing a child is the most unnatural and unimaginable of all losses. It's simply not the natural order of things. Children aren't supposed to die before their parents, regardless of age. Upon losing a child, many parents find themselves alternating between excruciating pain and numbness. They find themselves merely existing from day-to-day. To do much more seems impossible.

A parent's whole existence seems to be wrapped up in their child, regardless of the child's age. Your whole life is dedicated to living for, loving, caring for, and protecting that child. Suddenly, they're no longer there. Though it is far more common than you might imagine, it is tragic beyond comprehension. The injustice of the death of a child creates a loss that is, at least in our experience, not only life-changing but life-shattering.

Miscarriage and Stillbirth

When a baby dies before birth, it's just as devastating. The problem is that people don't seem to take it as seriously as the mother and father do. The whole reality of the baby hadn't hit them yet as it had hit you. They didn't hold the baby or feel them kick or move in the womb. They didn't nourish your child or have wonderful thoughts for his or her future. You did. And just as with the loss of any child, you will experience grief. You may go through denial, anger, depression, or the other stages of grief. You may blame yourself, the doctor, or even God.

Guilt is common after a miscarriage or stillbirth. Many parents blame themselves. You must realize that it's not your fault. You did nothing wrong. Do not blame yourself. If you have not suffered such a thing, I believe it is quite literally impossible to understand. Losing those you love -whether 100 or still in the womb is tragic and beyond description.

In all of the above scenarios and countless others, I have no answers except to trust God. There is no other answer. Even in this trust, you will endure the pain and suffering that comes with loss. Faith in our creator does, however, give us hope.

How the Marriage is Affected

Remember that no two people grieve the same. This is true for married couples as well. This confusion and misunderstanding can cause volatility in a marriage, especially when coupled with the frustration, anger, blame, and guilt of a child's death. It's vital that the parents share their feelings and openly communicate throughout the grieving process.

The great news is that, despite common belief, most couples do not divorce after the death of a child. In fact, only about 12-16% of divorces are related to the loss of a child. Perhaps if there were more understanding about the grief process, this rate would be lower.

How can I Possibly get Over the Loss of my Child?

You won't! You will never get over the loss of a child. I wish there was more encouraging news. This is simply too momentous to ever get over. That's the bad news. The good news is that while you will never get over the loss of your child, you can get through it. In fact, you may one day even experience joy again. It will never be the same as the ugly monster of grief will always be there, lurking in the background. Grief will, however, have less influence on your life as the years go by. There will be brief little moments of happiness shining through over time like a momentary sun ray through the storm clouds. It will come. It will not be easy, and it will not be fast, but it is as inevitable as the rising of the sun each morning

The following tools may be of help for some when specifically coping with parental grief.

Take Small Steps

It's vital to take life one step at a time after the death of a child. Life may seem unbearable, but if you focus on one step at a time, you will get through it.

Keep a Journal

There will be some things that you just can't express to anyone. Write these thoughts down. Some people write their journals as a letter to their children. This is healing for them.

Accept Happiness

Sometimes, parents mistakenly believe that they betray their children if they allow themselves to enjoy life again. They become unable even to acknowledge that pleasure exists. You must realize that it's okay to laugh amid tears. You're not abandoning your grief by laughing. The only way to survive your grief is to step away from it for a moment.

Remember the Positive Moments

Rather than focusing on the death of your child, focus on the good times you had together. Remember the joyous times in their life. Look at pictures. Consider making a journal of the good times that you can remember. Look at their baby book. Reminisce about the good times.

Share Your Needs

Lastly, let your support system know what you need. That's what they are there for. They want to help, but they can't help if they don't know what you need.

Losing a Parent

Your parent—the person you have known and loved longer than any other, the person who shaped you into who you are is gone. Losing a parent means so much to so many. Some of our best (or worst) memories are linked to our parents. The death of a parent forever alters the security of our childhood and the very foundation of our lives. It creates a void in our life no other person can fill. Yet, because losing a parent is one of the most common types of loss, many wrongly assume that such grief is easily overcome. In reality, nothing could be further from the truth. The loss of a parent represents the end of the single most enduring relationship of your life.

Unique Challenges

You are your parent's child, even as an adult. It's part of your identity and has been your whole life. Thus, even if you're an adult, when your parent passes, you may feel abandoned.

If your parent could not care for themselves and you were their primary caregiver, that can heighten those feelings. You have lost two roles. You were someone's child, and you were acting as a caregiver.

Changes in Relationships

When a parent dies, it can cause you to look at life differently. You may begin to realize that our time here is limited and start to value relationships more. You may begin to put more of a priority on the relationships in your life.

Losing a Sibling

The loss of a sibling often gets overlooked as nearly everyone else's loss seems to take precedence. When losing a sibling, especially during childhood, the surviving sibling is often closer to the deceased than anyone else. Growing up, siblings share everything—experiences, pets, clothing, memories, secrets, history, and a formative past. Siblings know each other in an extraordinary way, yet they seem to get overlooked after the loss.

Our youngest son lost both of his siblings, leaving him an only child. Looking back, we can see that he did indeed receive far less attention or recognition of his losses than we did. We, as parents, have friends who are also parents. It is far more natural to empathize when you have children of your own. The outpouring of love from our friends and church family was phenomenal for my wife and me.

Often a surviving sibling gets precious little in the way of individual attention. A sibling's peer group, especially when young, is not likely to have the emotional maturity to really "be there" when needed the most. Parents, overwhelmed by grief, often do not give the emotional support or inclusion needed. That was the sad reality of which we are not proud.

We gravely regret that we were not there as we should have been for Aaron. If you are reading this and have recently lost a sibling, we encourage you to reach out to your family and let them know how much this loss has hurt you. Your family loves you and aches for your loss too. Sometimes, the most important of relationships can get lost in grief.

How Children Are Affected.

Children who lose their siblings are adversely affected in several ways, including their health, schooling, behavior, development, and self-esteem. Many children who have lost their sibling grow up feeling lonely, sad, and "different." When you lose a sibling, you also lose a friend unlike any other. This is the friend you grew up with, the friend you fought with and still loved like no one else. The sibling order changes when a brother or sister passes. If the oldest sibling passed on, someone else is now the oldest, throwing that person into a different role.

A child is similar to an adult who loses a sibling in that they remember all the fights they've had, and they feel guilty over them. However, a child may see themselves as the bad sibling and the other sibling as the good one in each fight. This can result in misplaced feelings of guilt, regret, and even shame.

Parenting a Child Who Has Lost a Sibling

Because losing a child is so difficult, parents are often overwhelmed with their own grief and may forget to address the grief of the surviving sibling. A surviving child may feel like they need to "fill in" for the sibling that died. They may also worry that their parents wish they had died rather than their sibling. It's vital that parents recognize the surviving sibling's grief and support them.

Suicide

We are, unfortunately, intimately familiar with death by suicide as our oldest son took his own life. The death of a loved one at their own hands deals an incredibly personal and painful blow to the family left behind. Society's view of suicide and the survivor's feelings of betrayal and failure, in addition to the other common emotions that accompany death, make this an extremely painful loss to endure. The accompanying grief brings additional layers of pain and suffering. The burden of the stigma can keep survivors from getting much-needed support and resources. Those who lose a loved one to suicide are at higher risk of developing post-traumatic stress disorder, major depression, a prolonged form of grief called complicated grief, and suicidal behaviors themselves.

Suicide is, in and of itself, a subject for which entire books have been written. If there is anything more painful or harder to understand than the loss of a loved one, it would be the loss of a loved one who has chosen to take their own life. The questions are endless. Why didn't he love his children or us enough? Why didn't we see this coming? Why couldn't we help him? Did we do all we could to try to help her? What will people think? We can love them and still be angry with what has happened. Life is one big series of choices, and we are each responsible for our choices. No matter their circumstances, suicide was a choice. It was their choice, not yours. It is not your fault.

Unique Challenges

An estimated 85% of Americans will personally know someone who committed suicide in their lifetime. Suicide loss survivors often face challenges that are unique from those who encounter other forms of grief. These grievers often face confusion, overwhelming guilt, shame, rejection, and anger on top of the typical grief reactions. Besides this, they are faced with the effects of trauma and stigma. For this reason, those whose loved ones die by suicide have higher incidences of blaming, rejection, shame, and the need to hide the cause of death. Don't let the circumstances of your loved one's death hinder your grief process.

Survivors of loss due to suicide may develop post-traumatic stress disorder (PTSD) due to experiences associated with the suicide. Survivors are typically the ones to find their loved one's body and may even see the event take place. Thankfully, I did not see my son take his life, but finding his body was difficult enough. Suicides are commonly gruesome scenes to come upon. This is why PTSD is all too common in survivors.

Most survivors feel a burning need to understand what their loved one was thinking at the end of their life and why they made the decision they did. Survivors often believe themselves somehow responsible and feel guilty for not having done more to prevent it. They often dig through past events for every little clue they have missed that could have led them to see where their loved one was headed. Then, they blame themselves for not noticing or not taking the clues seriously enough when there was no way they could have known what was about to happen.

Survivors may feel abandoned by their loved ones. They may feel their loved one chose suicide over them or that they were rejected. They may also feel angry about it. These are normal feelings after a suicide.

Unlike the many other ways people die, suicide carries with it a stigma. This leaves those grieving feeling isolated. They feel unable to talk about the death of their loved one, unable to get counseling or support, and unwilling to join grief groups.

Support Groups

One "place" to get support is from other survivors through suicide support groups. You might find it beneficial to find a support group filled with those who have lost someone of a similar relation (i.e., everyone has lost their sibling to suicide as you have).

There are support groups facilitated by trained laypersons, who are often suicide survivors themselves, and others facilitated by mental health professionals. As long as you can open up without feeling judged, does it matter who's leading the group?

Support groups are available at any time. Some support groups meet online. It's never too early or too late to join a support group. Grief anniversaries pop up every year, making grief raw again. Reach out anytime you need to.

Professional Help

Some suicide survivors seek out a therapist. They find great help there. When seeking out a mental health professional, look for experience working with those grieving from loss after a suicide.

A therapist can help in many ways. They can help you explore unfinished issues in your relationship with your loved one and offer you understanding and support throughout your grief journey. They can also help you make sense of your loved one's death and help you better understand your loved one's psychiatric problems that may have led to their suicide. The therapist can help you cope with the reactions of your family and friends. Lastly, they can treat you if you have developed PTSD.

National Tragedy

Like the attack on September 11, 2001, or the Oklahoma City bombing, national tragedies create grief on many levels. Those who lost someone directly in the tragedy are affected, but even the very psyche of the entire nation is impacted.

Typical Reactions

Reactions to national and public tragedies typically display various responses (physically, emotionally, and cognitively). These reactions depend on several variables, including the survivor's support system, perceived ability to give and receive help, proximity to the event, cultural norms and values, prior psychological functioning, and more.

The event itself can cause overwhelming feelings of shock, panic, anger, guilt, depression, or grief. They may suffer confusion, flashbacks, forgetfulness, and have difficulty concentrating accompanied by fatigue, body pain, headaches, nausea, and more. They may even go through withdrawal, conflict, and feelings of rejection—and all of this without having lost anyone close to them. These feelings, however, may only last a short time.

Intense Reactions

Some people react intensely, however, and may need immediate care. These people have what is called the post-traumatic stress response. A few of the symptoms associated with this are:

- Hypersensitivity
- Flashbacks
- Panic attacks
- Severe Depression
- Suicidal thoughts
- Denial of the event

When a Loved One Passes

The initial reactions are only the start when a loved one has passed due to a national or public tragedy. The shock that everyone feels upon hearing that the disaster has occurred is generally short-lived. This is followed closely by overwhelming grief and severe separation anxiety. The person may begin searching for their loved one, even knowing that they have died.

Survivors may be at risk for complicated grief, especially if they cannot verify that their loved one has indeed died due to the nature of the tragedy, if the loved one was a child, or if the survivor has difficulty coping with adversity.

Ways to Cope

Joining a professionally led support group for victims of tragedy can be extremely helpful. Not only will it offer you support and a place to safely express your feelings when you need it most, but it will allow you to offer support to others so you can redirect your focus off yourself. All of these are vital. Learn to accept help from those who offer it. Even if you don't want to admit it, you can use the help right now, and they need to help right now; it may help those around you feel less helpless.

Get back into your regular routines, such as exercise and mealtimes, but don't make yourself adhere to the same strict schedule. Instead, find some way to enjoy yourself every day.

Lastly, I've stated this before, but it needs to be reiterated, don't make any major life decisions right away. Don't change jobs, relocate, or end any relationships until you can think rationally, and that may be a while. Give yourself time. You'll be in emotional upheaval for a bit. Be patient with yourself and others. Instead of making major life decisions based on your emotions, write your thoughts and feelings in a journal, express your thought in detail so you can come back to them later. Looking back on your thoughts at a later date can be helpful.

Pandemic (COVID-19)

There are many reasons for grief during this pandemic. Yes, people are grieving lives lost, and we'll get to that, but people are also grieving secondary losses. Secondary losses include the lost recreation, relationships, social support, and the inability to connect in a meaningful way over the last year. These things also bring grief that people haven't been prepared to experience. Added to the loss of life, the pandemic has been heart-wrenching for those left behind.

The horrific once-in-a-century event didn't just affect groups of people or even just one nation. It affected all of humanity. Unlike any other tragedy, our losses were suffered, for the most part, without collective mourning. In many cases, we weren't even permitted to be at the bedside of our dying loved ones. Funerals, kept to ten or less for the sake of health regulations, were unattended by many loved ones or attended virtually (later in the pandemic).

To make matters worse, many people choose to believe that COVID-19 is a farce, or some ridiculous government conspiracy set in motion to take over the nation. While this is clearly not the case, there are legitimate concerns with how this pandemic was handled, ranging from the Chinese governments original handling of the outbreak as well as the World Health Organization to determinations made as to cause of death in each case and, as always, the politicization of the pandemic. All have impacted our understanding of this horrible scourge on mankind. Consequently, many question the accuracy of those whose deaths can be attributed to the virus. For many, this has had the tragic underlying effect of denying their legitimacy and seemingly denying our right to grieve. So how do we grieve for those we lost during the pandemic?

How to Cope

Firstly, talk it out with friends and family who understand. If you have feelings that you don't feel comfortable expressing to others, write them in a journal. Regardless of how you do it, get them off your chest.

An online support group is always a great place to find people to talk to as well.

Because many of us could not attend the memorial service for our loved ones, you may have felt cheated in your grieving or simply feel it was not handled properly. Perhaps you could create a scrapbook celebrating your loved one's life.

Celebrate your loved ones by doing what you believe they would want you to do—take care of yourself. Eat well, get plenty of sleep, spend time in mindfulness exercises, and speak of exercise... dare I say it again? Even just a short walk each day in the sunshine will do wonders for the spirit.

Lastly, even if you don't feel like it, try to keep doing what you enjoy. Routine has a certain comfort to it that gives life its meaning.

Dementia/Alzheimer's

The slow loss of your loved one before your very eyes is a complicated and prolonged form of loss that fosters a type of grief that is equally complicated. This type of grief starts years before your loved one physically dies.

You are losing your loved ones before they die. They are becoming a shell of themselves. And the knowledge that they are "slowly passing" is a lot to bear. This is one of the reasons you start grieving their loss before you lose them entirely.

With other terminal illnesses, such as cancer and heart disease, you get to "keep" your loved ones with you until they pass. Dementia and Alzheimer's take them slowly yet relentlessly before your eyes. You still have their body to care for, but they're a whole different person, a person who doesn't recognize you anymore. Thus, comes pre-death grief.

Often, when a parent passes away who didn't recognize their children due to Alzheimer's or Dementia, the children find that their grief isn't as intense as they think it should be. This is typical because they have been grieving their parent already for many years. However, everyone is different. Some people still grieve very deeply. There are also times that pre-death grief can lead to complicated grief. We must be vigilant to observe both ourselves and others who might find themselves in such a situation.

Ways to Cope

Prepare yourself. You're likely to experience your feelings of loss and grief more than once as Dementia and Alzheimer's progresses. Think about those feelings. Accept them—the negative as well as the positive. You're grieving, and the conflicting emotions you feel are all part of that grieving process. Feel them and express them, whether it's out loud to yourself, to others, or on paper.

Don't isolate yourself. As a caregiver, you may be tempted to give up companionship and activities you enjoy, but you must combat those lonely feelings and those desires to isolate. Find someone to step in and watch your parent while you go on a lunch date with some friends. And don't make it a once-in-a-while thing, either. Make yourself stay involved in the things you enjoy!

Find an Alzheimer's support group near you and join it. They are all over the country. It is natural to discuss caregiving in these groups, but remember this time is for you to share your struggles and emotions. Support one another in this difficult journey. You probably need the support more than you realize.

Lastly, take care of yourself. Remember what you are capable of. Are you expecting too much of yourself? Control the things you can—eat well, get plenty of sleep, and do things that make you happy. Ask others to help you do those things that you're not capable of doing.

Types of Grief

G rief can be subcategorized into three areas: acute grief, integrated grief, and complicated grief. Acute grief is the initial instinctual reaction we have to losing a loved one. At some point, acute grief usually transitions into integrated grief, which is the ongoing grief you experience after adapting to the death of a loved one. You have entered integrated grief when you can begin to enjoy life, love, and think about your loved one with composure once again. It may take longer for someone to transition into integrated grief after a suicide.

Acute Grief

While we will identify different types of grief it is important to recognize that many of the symptoms, we experienced in the various types of grief may overlap. The duration and severity of those symptoms can vary quite a bit.

Some of the symptoms experienced in acute grief can also be symptoms of major medical emergencies. If you're not sure that the symptoms you or your loved one are experiencing are grief-related, then get medical attention right away.

The following is a list of possible Responses to Acute Grief

Physical Symptoms of Anxiety from Grief:

- Tightness in the throat
- Choking
- Shortness of breath
- Sighing
- An empty feeling in the stomach
- Lack of muscular strength
- Intense subjective distress described as tension or pain

Physical Symptoms of Grief

- Fatigue
- Trouble initiating or maintaining sleep
- Chest heaviness or pain
- Shortness of breath
- Tightness in the throat
- Palpitations
- Nausea Diarrhea
- Constipation
- Abdominal, stomach pain
- Back pain
- Headache
- Lightheaded, dizziness
- Change in appetite – increased or decreased
- Weight change
- Hair Loss
- Crying, sighing
- Restlessness

Emotional Symptoms

- Sadness
- Anger
- Irritability
- Relief
- Anxiety
- Panic
- Meaninglessness, Apathy
- Numbness
- Abandonment
- Helplessness
- Emotionally labile
- Vulnerability
- Self-Blame, Fear
- Guilt
- Longing
- Loneliness
- Apathy
- Disbelief
- Denial

Social Symptoms

- Overly sensitive
- Dependent
- Withdrawn
- Avoid others

- Lack of initiative
- Lack of interest
- Hyperactive
- Underactive
- Relationship difficulties
- Lowered self-esteem

Behavioral Symptoms

- Forgetfulness
- Difficulty concentrating
- Slowed thinking
- Sense of Unreality
- Wandering aimlessly
- Feeling trance-like
- Feelings of unreality
- Feelings of emptiness
- Dreams of the deceased
- Searching for the deceased
- Sense the loved one's presence
- Hallucinations of the deceased, sensing their presence (visual or auditory) Assuming mannerisms or traits of the loved one
- Needing to retell the story of the loved one's death
- Preoccupied with one's own death
- Avoiding talking about loss so others won't feel uncomfortable

Complicated Grief

As many as 10% of people cannot transition into integrated grief and experience an unresolved, prolonged, intense grief that stays fresh and raw regardless of the passing of time. This is known as complicated grief, which causes distress, the inability to function, and difficulty creating a meaningful life without their loved ones.

Other symptoms of complicated grief include:

- Preoccupation with their loved one
- Dramatically restricting their life to avoid all reminders of the loss
- Frequent intrusive images of their loved one's death
- Happy memories may be blocked out or misinterpreted as sad
- They may spend so much time thinking about their loved one that it interferes with daily activities
- Life feels empty
- Intense pangs of grief
- They may have such a strong desire to be with their loved ones that they begin to have suicidal thoughts and behaviors
- Their own death may begin to feel like the only relief available

Those with complicated grief have difficulty functioning occupationally, socially, and in their day-to-day life. They typically have higher rates of depression, PTSD, suicidal ideation, and suicidal behavior. Complicated grief can also affect a person's physical health. Untreated, complicated grief will not go away.

How Is Complicated Grief Treated?

Complicated grief does not need to be permanent. It can be professionally resolved. Treatment is approached in several ways.

Psychoeducation

One of the approaches is through psychoeducation. As a person learns more about death and mourning, it can help normalize their experiences since they have lost their loved ones. Being able to process the sudden or unexpected nature of the death can also help the griever to stop being preoccupied with it.

Cognitive Behavioral Therapy

Cognitive-behavioral therapy explores the faulty thinking that the survivor might be believing and helps them challenge that thinking. Those inaccurate thoughts can be interfering with the grief journey. Challenging those thoughts and changing them out for the right thoughts will aid in healing their complicated grief.

Group Therapy

The peer support and professional support provided through group therapy are a double win. The grieving individual gets help from others who are battling complicated grief while getting the aid of a professional.

Interpersonal Therapy

Interpersonal therapy focuses on helping the individual build healthier relationships with those people in their lives who are still alive. This can be helpful and adds more therapeutic outlets. Once they have closer relationships with the other people in their lives, they'll be able to communicate their feelings to them as well. They'll also be able to move forward with their life.

Personal Work

If someone is struggling with complicated grief, their therapist will also have them do personal work. A few things they might have them try are prayer or meditation, journaling, or building a support team.

If you think you might be struggling with complicated grief, please reach out to a mental health care professional today!

Integrated Grief

Integrated grief is the most enduring type of grief. As we begin to accept the meaning and reality of death, we are better able to begin living life once again. We begin to integrate the thoughts of our loved ones into our memory.

The human mind is a wonderfully complex and mysterious thing. We assume that memories consist only of facts and past events exactly as they happened. In reality, memories are constructed within our minds from a combination of past events and events exactly as we wish them to have been.

This helps us get to a place in our lives where every memory of our loss is no longer all-encompassing or disabling. We will still feel sad and even miss them. Eventually, we can experience fond memories alongside our sadness. We may, however, still have times when we momentarily slip back into more severe grief. For most of us, this is inevitable.

Integrated grief, while not ideal, is the most manageable and likely the type of grief we will live with for the rest of our lives. We would be foolish to imagine that we can run the gauntlet of grief and somehow cross the finish line never to look back. Integrated grief provides a precious balance between the sorrow of your loss that will always be with you and the joy of living.

Conclusion

The Odds are, we will all lose someone we love at some point in our life. And we will all grieve each person we lose in a different way.

Though there are five general stages of grief, grief is unique for everyone. None of us will experience these stages in the same way or order, with the same frequency, or on the exact timetable as anyone else. In fact, everyone may not experience every stage of grief, and some may experience each stage several times. Everyone's grief is unique.

While you're thrust into this cycle of grief, you're also thrown into the many practical issues that must be dealt with. This creates a flood of activities and responsibilities you're not ready for—finances, funeral arrangements, expense accounts, POA, insurance, bills, caring for your loved one's belongings, and more. And all of this comes at the worst possible time. Somehow, in the midst of all this, you must also take care of yourself, as grief affects your body and mind.

You must put yourself first, remembering to take care of yourself, interact with others, and do the things you love. You will face many emotions that you may not understand, but you must allow yourself to feel them if you are to heal from them in any way.

If you have picked up this book and come this far, you are grieving. Nothing in this book will change that reality. No words, no person, no plan, or process can change what you are experiencing. Unlike our society, where there is generally a pill for what ails you, there is no magic potion. That is the plain ugly hard truth of it. Tremendous sorrow and grief have become unwelcome travel companions, and it looks like they brought plenty of baggage for the trip. To indicate anything less would be simply spewing falsehoods that would prove to be utterly useless with time. That is the complicated but inescapable truth of grief. What you are going through is unique to you and you alone, and it is a journey you must travel, for the most part, on your own. You already know this is true, but it can be freeing to accept.

To care for others is to be truthful, even when it is not what they want to hear. Understanding and accepting this new reality is an essential step towards finding peace again.

When a wild horse first experiences the burden of weight and unwanted influence of a human rider, they will buck and fight, making the burden they have been forced to carry all the more unbearable. Eventually, the horse decides to accept the inevitable and stops trying so hard to change the fact that they now have a new burden that they must contend with from time to time. As that realization sets in, life with this uninvited intruder becomes more and more bearable. The day eventually comes when they are so used to this extra weight that it no longer seems to bother them. They settle into their new routine and find contentment in their new circumstances. We also must come to that place of acceptance. Life will never be the same. That does not, however, have to mean that it will never again be worth living.

Nothing is the same, and that is okay. You will not be the same. That is okay too. You will grow. Using the tools in this book, you will be stronger. Now, go use them!

If you enjoyed this book, please leave a review on Amazon.

DOWNLOADABLE THINGS TO DO CHECKLIST

We have made available a downloadable pdf of "Things to Do" at the link below to help you track and plan. Remember that this is not an exhaustive list, and it may include items that don't pertain to you. It is just a practical guide and checklist, designed to help organize and remind you of things you may need to do. If you are reading this book later in your journey, you may not need this resource. If, however, your loss is more recent, then you may find this to be a valuable source. If you know of someone suffering a loss, please feel free to download and pass it along if you feel comfortable. The purpose of this book, after all, is to help as many grieving people as possible. Use the QRC below.

Resource and Support Section

- Resources for Help: https://www.verywellmind.com/best-online-grief-support-groups-4842333

- Best Overall: https://forums.grieving.com/

- Best Live Chat: https://www.griefincommon.com/

- Best for Young People: https://www.hopeagain.org.uk/

- Best Social Media Group: https://griefanonymous.com/facebook-groups/

- Best for Specific Grief:

  http://www.onlinegriefsupport.com/groups

- Best for Email Support:

  https://www.griefnet.org/support/SGform.html

- Best Monitored Discussion Group:

  https://www.griefhealingdiscussiongroups.com/

About the Authors

Ron and Jeff have both experienced significant losses in unexpected ways. Jeff lost his father in a tragic industrial accident at the tender age of 18 months old.

While too young to remember the actual day of his father's accident, Jeff experienced the never-ending consequences of the loss of his dad. As the child of a widowed mom, his entire childhood was continually shaped by that loss. His mom did not handle the loss of her husband well and spent years on medications just to make it through the days. Consequently, Jeff suffered not only the loss of his dad but, for all practical purposes, his mom as well. With his mother unable to cope, Jeff bounced around between his aunt and uncle and his grandfather until he was seven or eight years old.

Ron suffered the loss of his father when he was 19 years old. His dad died of pancreatic cancer at the age of 47. He would subsequently marry and have three boys. He lost his oldest son Adam to suicide when his son was only 27 years old. Still reeling from the loss of his firstborn child, he would lose his second eldest son, Eric, in the line of duty leaving behind a wife and four young children. His son was a sergeant in the infantry.

Jeff's loss of his father at such a tender young age and the years that followed as he watched his mother struggle with the use of prescription medication in an attempt to numb the pain of their loss gives Jeff a unique view of loss and the impact it has on so many.

Ron's struggle with grief began as a young man with the loss of his father. The death of his children has given Ron tremendous compassion and understanding for the depth of suffering and difficulty death brings.

Ron and Jeff have lived with the aftermath of the death of multiple family members for many years. Their collective experience with grief spans over 80 years and has given them an insight into grief that makes them uniquely qualified to help others.

References

- 16 ideas for creating new holiday tradition after a death. What's your Grief. (2021, April 12). https://whatsyourgrief.com/creating-new-tradition-after-a-death/.

- 19 worst things to say to a Grieving person. Amen Clinics 19 Worst Things to Say to a Grieving Person Comments. (n.d.). https://www.amenclinics.com/blog/19-worst-things-to-say-to-a-grieving-person/.

- 4 tips to deal with people who say the wrong thing when YOU'RE GRIEVING. What's your Grief? (2021, April 12). https://whatsyourgrief.com/people-say-the-wrong-thing-grief/.

- 6 ways to Manage grief and rebuild your life after a loss. Sixty and Me. (2020, May 25). https://sixtyandme.com/6-ways-to-manage-grief-and-rebuild-your-life-after-a-loss.

- Advanced Solutions International, I. (n.d.). Grieving the loss of a child. https://www.aamft.org/Consumer_Updates/Grieving_the_Loss_of_A_Child.aspx.

- Alan D. Wolfelt, P. D. (n.d.). Helping yourself heal when your spouse dies. GriefWords.com. https://griefwords.com/index.cgi?action=page&page=articles%2Fhelping3.html&site_id=2.

- Alzheimer's disease and 'the long goodbye'. Alzheimer's Disease Research Center. (n.d.). https://www.adrc.pitt.edu/alzheimers-disease-and-the-long-goodbye/.

- American Psychological Association. (n.d.). Recovering emotionally from disaster. American Psychological Association. https://www.apa.org/topics/disasters-response/recovering.

- Blandin, K., & Pepin, R. (2017, January). Dementia grief: A theoretical model of a unique grief experience. Dementia

(London, England).
https://www.ncbi.nlm.nih.gov/pmc/articles/PMC4853283/.

- Burns, L. (2020, July 2). Elisabeth Kübler-Ross: The rise and fall of the five stages of grief. BBC News. https://www.bbc.com/news/stories-53267505.

- Busch, M. (n.d.). Do we move on or move forward from grief? Do We Move On or Move Forward From Grief? https://www.buschcares.com/blog/do-we-move-on-or-move-forward-from-grief.

- By, Sage on "> at said: Crystal on "> at said: Jade on "> at said: Anya on "> at said: & Eric on "> at said: (n.d.). Avoiding the pitfalls of grief isolation. GriefandMourning.com | Grief is itself a medicine. https://griefandmourning.com/avoiding-the-pitfalls-of-grief-isolation.

- Closure isn't a thing in grief and that's okay. What's your Grief. (2021, June 24). https://whatsyourgrief.com/closure-isnt-a-thing-in-grief-and-thats-okay/.

- Common grief reactions. Hospice of the Red River Valley. (2020, October 1). https://www.hrrv.org/grief-support/common-grief-reactions/.

- Coping with change after a loss. Cancer.Net. (2019, October 18). https://www.cancer.net/coping-with-cancer/managing-emotions/grief-and-loss/coping-with-change-after-loss.

- Coping with grief during a pandemic. Penn Foundation. (2020, July 20). https://www.pennfoundation.org/news-events/articles-of-interest/coping-with-grief-during-a-pandemic/.

- Coping with loss and grief during covid-19. Cedars. (n.d.). https://www.cedars-sinai.org/blog/coping-with-loss-and-grief-during-covid-19.html.

- Coping with public tragedies and natural disasters. Coping With Public Tragedies & Natural Disasters | VITAS Healthcare. (n.d.).

https://www.vitas.com/family-and-caregiver-support/grief-and-bereavement/coping-with-grief/coping-with-public-tragedies-and-natural-disasters.

- Dealing with anger and resentment with loss. Willwerscheid Funeral Home and Cremation - Serving St. Paul and West St. Paul Minnesota. (2020, January 9). https://willwerscheid.com/2020/01/09/resentment-in-loss/.

- The death of a spouse. The Grief Recovery Method. (n.d.). https://www.griefrecoverymethod.com/blog/2017/02/death-spouse.

- Devine, M. (2014, February 10). Why we need to change our approach to grief. HuffPost. https://www.huffpost.com/entry/stages-of-grief_b_4414077.

- Devine, M. (2020, January 29). The secret side of grief: The culture of blame. BEST SELF. https://bestselfmedia.com/grief-blame/.

- Edelman, H. (2021, February 26). Opinion | pandemic grief could become its own health crisis. The Washington Post. https://www.washingtonpost.com/opinions/2021/02/26/pandemic-grief-could-become-its-own-health-crisis/.

- Free guide: After death checklist - the legacy lawyers. Legacy Lawyers. (2020, May 1). https://www.thelegacylawyers.com/free-guides/after-death-checklist/.

- Gillihan, S. J. (2019, July 11). How to avoid saying the wrong thing to someone grieving. WebMD. https://blogs.webmd.com/mental-health/20190711/how-to-avoid-saying-the-wrong-thing-to-someone-grieving.

- Grief and isolation. Whats your Grief. (2020, April 16). https://whatsyourgrief.com/grief-and-loneliness/.

- Grief and lingering feelings of resentment. Bertram's Blog. (2013, March 15). https://bertramsblog.com/2013/03/14/grief-and-lingering-feelings-of-resentment/.

- Grief and loss as alzheimer's progresses. Alzheimer's Disease and Dementia. (n.d.). https://www.alz.org/help-support/caregiving/caregiver-health/grief-loss-as-alzheimers-progresses#:~:text=Alzheimer's%20gradually%20takes%20away%20the,stages%20as%20time%20goes%20on.

- Grieving the death of a child is often referred to as the ultimate tragedy. HealGrief. (n.d.). https://healgrief.org/grieving-the-death-of-a-child/.

- Grieving the death of a parent can be a life-changing experience. HealGrief. (n.d.). https://healgrief.org/grieving-the-death-of-a-parent/.

- Grieving the death of a sibling is one of the most neglected types of grief. HealGrief. (n.d.). https://healgrief.org/grieving-the-death-of-a-sibling/.

- Grieving the death of a spouse...you can't get them out of your mind. HealGrief. (n.d.). https://healgrief.org/grieving-the-death-of-a-spouse/.

- Grieving the loss of a sibling. Cancer.Net. (2019, January 8). https://www.cancer.net/coping-with-cancer/managing-emotions/grief-and-loss/grieving-loss-sibling#:~:text=Grief%20is%20a%20normal%20response,parents%2C%20spouse%2C%20or%20children.

- Guilt and grief: Coping with the coulda, woulda, shouldas. Whats your Grief. (2020, April 16). https://whatsyourgrief.com/guilt-and-grief-2/.

- Guilt and regret - TRANSITIONS lifecare Bereavement Blog. Transitions LifeCare. (2020, January 24). https://transitionslifecare.org/2020/01/29/guilt-and-regret/.

- Guttmacher, B. C. (2011, September). Advice and Care for Caregivers. Washington, DC; www.chordomafoundation.org.
- Hairston, S. (2019, July 11). How grief shows up in your body. WebMD. https://www.webmd.com/special-reports/grief-stages/20190711/how-grief-affects-your-body-and-mind.
- How suicide bereavement is different. Survivors of Bereavement by Suicide. (n.d.). https://uksobs.org/for-professionals/how-suicide-bereavement-is-different/.
- How to overcome grief's health-damaging effects. Harvard Health. (2021, February 15). https://www.health.harvard.edu/mind-and-mood/how-to-overcome-griefs-health-damaging-effects.
- Institute of Medicine (US) Committee on Palliative and End-of-Life Care for Children and Their Families. (1970, January 1). Bereavement experiences after the death of a child. When Children Die: Improving Palliative and End-of-Life Care for Children and Their Families. https://www.ncbi.nlm.nih.gov/books/NBK220798/.
- Jacobs, B. J. (2015, June 8). Caregivers feeling relief and grief simultaneously. AARP. https://www.aarp.org/caregiving/life-balance/info-2017/relief-guilt-caregiving-ends.html.
- Krisch, J. A. (2021, June 10). Losing a parent changes us forever. there's proof. Fatherly. https://www.fatherly.com/health-science/parent-death-psychological-physical-effects/.
- Kubitz, M., & 17, M. K. on A. (2020, May 26). What is strength in the face of grief? Alive in Memory. https://www.aliveinmemory.org/2015/04/17/what-is-strength-in-the-face-of-grief/#.YGNiD69KiUk.
- Long, C. by E. (2019, May 24). 4 things you need to know about 'MOVING ON' from grief. GoodTherapy.org Therapy Blog.

https://www.goodtherapy.org/blog/4-things-you-need-to-know-about-moving-on-from-grief-0623155.

- Marshall, L. (2016, April 28). There's no right way to grieve. WebMD. https://www.webmd.com/mental-health/features/grieve-no-right-way.

- Mayo Foundation for Medical Education and Research. (2020, November 14). Grief: Coping with reminders after a loss. Mayo Clinic. https://www.mayoclinic.org/healthy-lifestyle/end-of-life/in-depth/grief/art-20045340.

- Melinda. (2021, June 14). Coping with grief and loss. HelpGuide.org. http://www.helpguide.org/articles/grief/coping-with-grief-and-loss.htm.

- Mendoza, M. (2016, June 17). The Worst Things to Say to Someone Who's Mourning [web log]. https://www.psychologytoday.com.

- Mental health, grief and bereavement. Playbook. (n.d.). https://disasterplaybook.org/strategies/mental-health-grief-and-bereavement/.

- Nall, R. (2017, December 8). Depression after the death of a loved one. Healthline. https://www.healthline.com/health/depression/death-loved-one#when-to-see-a-doctor.

- Next Avenue. (2016, August 23). The life-challenging anguish of tidying up. Next Avenue. https://www.nextavenue.org/possessions-after-loved-ones-death/.

- Orbits, R. (n.d.). Ashley Davis BUSH, LICSW. Ashley Davis Bush. http://www.ashleydavisbush.com/articles/grief/the-myth-of-closure/.

- Rachael BenjaminA trained and passionate musician, Benjamin, R., & musician, A. trained and passionate. (2018, March 28). The death of a sibling changes everything. Tribeca Therapy.

https://tribecatherapy.com/5204/the-death-of-a-sibling-changes-everything/.

- Raymond, C. (2020, March 24). How grief can affect different parts of your body. Verywell Mind. https://www.verywellmind.com/physical-symptoms-of-grief-4065135.

- Reconnecting with life after Loss (one step at a time). Whats your Grief. (2020, April 16). https://whatsyourgrief.com/reconnecting-with-life-after-loss/.

- Relief after a death: The unspoken grief emotion. Whats your Grief. (2020, April 16). https://whatsyourgrief.com/relief-after-a-death-the-unspoken-emotion/.

- says, B., Buyviagra, says, J., Jan, says, N., Noelle, says, D. B., Brother, D., says, C., Cassie, says, K. L., Lucas, K., says, V., Vesna, Says, S., Sandy, says, C., Carol, says, M., … Terry. (2020, December 30). Is it time to "get back to life"? Grief doesn't work that way. Refuge In Grief. https://refugeingrief.com/2018/03/06/back-to-life/.

- says:, C. H., & says:, G. C. (2019, April 9). Death guilt: I feel like it's my fault. Grief Compass. https://griefcompass.com/deathguilt.

- Sewell, N. (2020, November 26). These four things are getting in the way of your grief. Nikki Sewell LCSW. https://milfordgrieftherapist.com/blog/guilt-and-shame-are-getting-in-the-way-of-your-grief.

- Sussex Publishers. (n.d.). The function of anger and resentment. Psychology Today. https://www.psychologytoday.com/us/blog/anger-in-the-age-entitlement/201812/the-function-anger-and-resentment.

- Sussex Publishers. (n.d.). Three ways to Address guilt when YOU'RE GRIEVING. Psychology Today.

https://www.psychologytoday.com/us/blog/supersurvivors/20200
6/three-ways-address-guilt-when-you-re-grieving.

- Sussex Publishers. (n.d.). Why do we punish ourselves?
  Psychology Today.
  https://www.psychologytoday.com/us/blog/the-squeaky-
  wheel/201407/why-do-we-punish-ourselves.

- Sussex Publishers. (n.d.). Why losing a parent hurts so much, no
  matter your age. Psychology Today.
  https://www.psychologytoday.com/us/blog/where-science-meets-
  the-steps/201709/why-losing-parent-hurts-so-much-no-matter-
  your-age.

- Tal Young, I., Iglewicz, A., Glorioso, D., Lanouette, N., Seay, K.,
  Ilapakurti, M., & Zisook, S. (2012, June). Suicide bereavement
  and complicated grief. Dialogues in clinical neuroscience.
  https://www.ncbi.nlm.nih.gov/pmc/articles/PMC3384446/.

- U.S. Department of Health and Human Services. (n.d.). Mourning
  the death of a spouse. National Institute on Aging.
  https://www.nia.nih.gov/health/mourning-death-spouse.

- Watch, H. W. H. (2020, June 15). Suicide survivors face grief,
  questions, challenges [web log]. https://www.health.harvard.edu/.

- What to do when Someone Dies: A checklist. Ever Loved. (n.d.).
  https://everloved.com/articles/end-of-life-affairs/what-to-do-
  when-someone-dies-checklist/.

- You're not suffering one loss, you're suffering many. VITAS
  Healthcare. (n.d.). https://www.vitas.com/family-and-caregiver-
  support/grief-and-bereavement/what-is-grief/suffering-loss.

- Bertmen SL, Sumpter HK, Greene HL. Bereavement and Grief.
  Chapter 219 in Greene HL (ed.) Clinical Medicine 2nd ed. St.
  Louis, MO: Mosby Year Book, Inc. 1996, pp. 856-8.

- Casarett D, Kutner JS, Abrahm J. Life after Death: A Practical
  Approach to Grief and Bereavement. Ann Intern Med

2001;134:208-215. Available at:
http://www.annals.org/issues/v134n3/full/200102060-00012.html

- Kutner JS. Grief and Bereavement: Physical, Psychological, and Behavioral Aspects. ACP Annual Meeting 2000. Available at: http://www.acponline.org/vas2000/sessions/grief.htm

- Hughes M. Bereavement and Support. Taylor & Francis, 1995.

- Saindon C. Grief: A Normal and Natural Response to Loss. Self Help Magazine. April 15, 1998. Available at: http://www.shpm.com/articles/trauma/grief.html

- Fitzgerald H. The Mourning Handbook. New York, N. Y.: A Fireside Book, 1994, p. 37.

- The acute responses to loss are not unhealthy or maladaptive responses. Rather they are normal responses to an abnormal event. Kirsti A. Dyer, MD, MS

- See the Emergency 911 Page for links to immediate resources if you are feeling helpless, hopeless, overwhelmingly depressed, or suicidal.

Made in the USA
Middletown, DE
19 June 2022

67396338R00113